Thomas Hooker

Preacher, Founder, Democrat; Biography of the Puritan Leader of Colonial New England

By George Leon Walker

Logo art adapted from work by Bernard Gagnon

ISBN-13: 978-0-359-74924-9

First published in 1891

Contents

Preface.......... v
Chapter One - Birth and Boyhood Associations.......... 6
Chapter Two - Education and Residence at Cambridge.......... 14
Chapter Three - Hooker's English Ministry.......... 20
Chapter Four - Life in Holland and Departure for America.......... 31
Chapter Five – In Massachusetts and Removal to Connecticut.......... 40
Chapter Six - Hooker in Connecticut.......... 51
Chapter Six - Hooker in Connecticut, Section II.......... 63
Chapter Six - Hooker in Connecticut. Section III.......... 71
Chapter Seven - Thomas Hooker's Writings.......... 81
Appendix One - Thomas Hooker's Will and Inventory of Estate 94
Appendix Two - Thomas Hooker's Published Works.......... 96

Preface

One striking difference in the advantages possessed by a biographer of the more distinguished personages of the Massachusetts and of the Connecticut colonies is the comparative destitution, in the latter case, of the aids afforded by contemporaneous diaries, histories, and portraits. The lack of such writings in the Connecticut annals is a little surprising; the want of portraits may be considerably accounted for by the remoter and poorer conditions of the inland settlement.

No portrait or other contemporaneous representation of Mr. Hooker remains. The picture which prefaces this volume is taken from Niehaus's statue, ordered by the Commonwealth of Connecticut for the State Capitol; in the making of which the artist compared the likenesses of various and widely separated members of Mr. Hooker's lineal posterity, among whom exists, however, a strong family resemblance. Attired thus in the characteristic costume of the time, the figure affords a not improbably fair representation of the great Founder of the Colony.

The present writer had occasion, in 1884, in narrating the two hundred and fifty years' history of the Hartford Church, of which Mr. Hooker was the first pastor, to publish, in a volume of local imprint and limited circulation, together with the biographies of subsequent pastors, the story of Mr. Hooker also. Subsequent repeated visits to the scenes of Mr. Hooker's English ministrations, as well as investigations at home, have added to the facts there narrated. Still, in addressing on the same theme the wider constituency of the Makers of America series, the writer could not, without awkwardness and even affectation, avoid the frequent use of language in which he had already narrated the same biographical and historical incidents. He has therefore drawn without hesitation on his own previous statements, so far as the altered proportions of a separate biography and added facts and illustrations suited him to do.

The valuable bibliography of Mr. Hooker's published writings (found in Appendix II.) was compiled by J. Hammond Trumbull, LL.D., to whom indebtedness is due, also, for the discovery and rescue from oblivion of the most important manuscript documents illustrative of Mr. Hooker's chief title to remembrance.

Hartford, Conn.,
September 1. 1891.

Chapter One - Birth and Boyhood Associations

Come, Hooker, *come forth of thy native soile.*
Johnson: *Wonder-Working Providence,* 1654.

Thomas Hooker was born at Marfield in Leicester County, England, probably on July 7, 1586. This little hamlet of Marfield — variously spelled in Leicester records as Mardifeud, Mardefelde, Markfelde, Markfild, Marefield, as well as Marfield — is one of four tithings which make up the parish of Tilton, or *Tilton super montem,* as the old chronicles often have it; the other three being Tilton, Halstead, and Whatborough. These four tithings or towns have for their common place of worship the stately gray-stone church of St. Peter, dating from the days of King John, built on the hill-top corner of the Tilton precinct of the parish, and commanding one of the widest and most beautiful landscape-views of Midland England. Around the church lies the churchyard, with four gates giving access to the four precincts of the ground allotted as a burial-place to the inhabitants of the four tithings which constitute the parish. The church itself is an interesting specimen of Early English architecture, with embattled tower, surmounted by an old, but later added spire, pierced by eight open windows, — a landmark visible from far. The word "steeple-chase" is said to be of Leicester County origin, and to have been derived from the many spires surmounting the hill-tops of this county, toward some one of which, in default of game, the disappointed hunters directed their chase; the first to gain which was accounted victor as if he had been "in at the death" of fox or deer.

It is with a feeling of surprise that one sees so stately and beautiful an edifice in so comparatively quiet and solitary a spot. Four ancient bells hang in the tower, — three of them bearing the inscription *I. H, S. Nazarenvs. Rex. Ivdeorvm. Fili. Dei. Misere. Mei.;* and one, of somewhat later date, the motto, *Praise the Lord.* These bells doubtless in former times summoned a far larger congregation to worship in the house below them than they can have gathered for several centuries past. The Wars of the Roses did much, in the two hundred years before the period at which our story begins, to depopulate the whole region; but the wonder still remains here, as well as in many other parts of England, how such churches as the traveller finds in the quietest and most secluded portions of the land could have been built amid so sparse a population as at any time lived on the soil about them.

But in young Hooker's day matters in this respect of numbers attendant on the services of the parish church could not have been much different from their condition at present. Twenty-two years before he was born a parliamentary return gives the number of houses in Tilton as twenty-eight, in

Halstead as sixteen, in Whatborough one, and in "Markfield" six. To-day Marfield has five; though as late as 1882 the present writer saw some carved beams which had belonged to another. These however, on a later examination, in 1886, were found to have been destroyed.

The visitor to the region, therefore, may be confident that he sees all things substantially as they were when the boyish eyes of young Thomas Hooker looked upon them. The picturesque old church of mottled gray on Tilton hill-top, compassed round by the dead of the different precincts of the parish; the wide prospect of alternating woodland and open fields and spire-surmounted hills toward every compass-point; the old *Rose and Crown* Inn, which Cromwell made his head-quarters when his army lay in this vicinity; the thatch-covered houses which hang irregularly around the summit occupied by the church and its Acre of God; and the little Marfield hamlet embowered in trees down in the valley, about a mile and a half away, and approached through rustic gates and stiles which the visitor opens or climbs as he descends through the sweet green fields, — all present a spectacle which cannot be materially different from the aspect it wore two and three hundred years ago.

Of the family ancestors of Thomas Hooker there is at present little known. His father, Thomas, appears to have come to Marfield from Blaston in the same county, in some capacity as overseer of the large landed properties of the Digby family; and as his grandfather bore the Christian name of "Kenellyme," it seems to be indicated that the connection with the Digby family, with whom Kenelm was a frequently recurrent name, must have been of long standing. The records of Tilton parish previous to 1610 having disappeared, it is impossible to state the date of young Thomas's birth or baptism. His mother, "Mrs. Hooker wife to Mr. Hooker of Marefield was buryed," April, 1631; his father, "Thomas Hooker of Marefield was buried" July 24, 1635; and his brother "Mr. John Hooker of Marfeild were burryed" Jan. 25, 1654. These are all the references to the family which appear on the extant records of the parish. But the title "Mr.," used in mention both of the father and brother of our Thomas, indicates that the family was regarded as of honourable standing. The will of the brother John, above mentioned, dated Jan. I, 1654-5, a few days before he died, and proved at London on November 26 of the same year, as the will of "John Hooker of Marfield, Co. Leicester, Gentleman," gives the same impression of recognized social position. This will bequeaths to "Samuel Hooker, student in New England, £100;" and to "John Hooker, student at Oxford, £200." These were the two sons of our Thomas, who at the date of this will had been some seven years dead in Hartford. The first named, Samuel, was then about graduating at Harvard College, and soon — in 1661 — to be minister at Farmington; and the other, John, was our Thomas's oldest son, of whom his dying father said in his will, July 7, 1647, "However I do not forbid my Sonne John from seeking and taking a wife in England, yet I doe forbid him from marrying and tarrying there." The young man did however marry and tarry there, and became a minister of the Episcopal church, rector of Lechamposted in Bucks, dying in 1684. There were also in the Marfield family of our Thomas's father at least four daughters, one of whom married a "revolutionist by the name of Pymm;" another, Frances, married a Tarlton of London; another, Dorothy, married John Chester of Blaby, Leicester County; and another married Mr. John Alcock, aftenvard deacon of the church in Roxbury, Massachusetts. Who the mother was who presided over the crowded household in the little Marfield home is at present unknown. Little can be recorded of her save that she lived long enough to see one of her boys become a preacher sufficiently famous to attract crowds whenever he spoke at the great parish-church of Leicester twelve miles away, to know of his exile to Holland, and to mourn the death [1] of one of her daughters in that far American land to which that son was still some years later to flee.

The family life at Marfield may have been comfortable and happy, but it must have been narrow and limited. Its chief points of interest, outside the concerns of home and the labours by which home wants were provided for, must have been in the church.

Even the material edifice which lifted itself as the most prominent object before the eye, contained many things suited to touch duller imaginations than young Thomas certainly had, or than were possessed probably by the whole group of brothers and sisters to whom the old building on the hill must have been at once the home of their fancy and their faith.

There was the quaint octagonal font at which had been baptized the generations of Tilton's parishioners from near the days of the Conquest. There were the monumental effigies of Jehan de Digbie and his wife; he a crusader — lying cross-legged with hand on his half-drawn sword, at his feet a lion — who died in 1269, and whose stone likeness was laid here not long after, with an inscription in old Norman French asking prayers; she, full-robed, large-moulded, lying by his side, a lap-dog at her feet. There, too, was another of the same family of a later generation, great-grandfather of a boy six years older than Thomas Hooker was, — which boy young Thomas might sometimes have seen at Tilton, where so much of the family property lay, — great-grandfather, that is to say, of Sir Everard Digby of the Gunpowder Plot, executed in St. Paul's churchyard in 1606. This old ancestor of the youth who was to attain so sinister an eminence lay there in coat-of-mail, a fleur-de-lis on his shield; having just before his death executed his will: "I bequeathe my sowle to God all myghty, our blessed lady Seynt Mary and all the Seynts of heven, my boddie to be buryed in the parishe church of Seynt Peter at Tilton, before the Ymcige of the blessed Trinitie att our Lady authur." Other monuments and escutcheons were there beside, to waken inquiry and to freshen fireside-legend and romantic tale.

Who the vicar of the parish was in Hooker's boyhood is probably only learned from a broken brass tablet in the church at Knossington, recording the burial-place of "Thomas Bayle...sometime rector of Tilton; "who, because we know who came before and after him, may with considerable likelihood be believed to have been the minister by whom Hooker was baptized. Vicar Bayle was succeeded by Christopher Denne. Little is known of him, except that he was the Tilton rector in 1610, and was probably a young man, as he had children christened between then and 1613, as shown by the parish records.

But concerning another minister of the parish in Hooker's early manhood, and for several years before his brother John's burial in the Marfield grave-plot, there is quite definite information. It is a sort of information, moreover, which sheds a good deal of light, not only on the religious condition of that parish, but on that of the important county of Leicester and of the country generally.

In the Minute-books of the Parliamentary Committee of Sequestration in the Bodleian Library, it is recorded, under date of 1645-6, that "Thomas Silverwood, minister to the Assembly, is referred to the church at Tilton." An entry of a later date, 1647, explains matters: "Whereas the Vicarage of the parish of Tilton, in the County of Leicester, is, and standeth, sequestrated by the Committee of Parliament from Dr. Manwaring for his delinquency, it is ordered that the said Vicarage shall stand and be sequestrated to the use henceforth of Thomas Silverwood, a godly and orthodox divine, and appointed to officiate said cure by the said Committee of Parliament." The nature of Dr. Manwaring's "delinquency" appears from the report of the Parliamentary Survey of the Churches in Leicester County, on which the action of the Parliament in "sequestrating" one minister "from" and another "to" the livings of the various Leicester parishes is based. That report divides the Leicester County ministers into "three sorts," — first, "Preachers," of whom there were one hundred and fifty-three; second, "No Preachers," by which is meant "no preaching and dumb ministers," as those who could or would only conduct service by the use of a liturgy were called, and of these there were seventy-six; third, "scandalous of both the former sorts, and they are 32." The report further divides the first-mentioned "sort" of ministers in Leicester, namely, "Preachers," into four classes, — "sufficient, 102; weak and unprofitable, 25; careless and negligent, 20; corrupt and unsound, 6."

The particular incumbent of the Tilton vicarage is set down as "no preacher and a pluralitan," from which the inference is that the Tilton vicar was an anti-Puritan or perhaps high prelatical man, who insisted on confining himself to the liturgy of the church and declined to preach, and that he held some other living beside that of Tilton. That he was "Dr." Manwaring — as well as Prebendary of Weeford, as is ascertainable from another source than the parliamentary statement about him — suggests that his "no preaching" depended rather upon his will than his ability; making him to differ in this respect from a great many of the clergy of the day, whose pulpit incapacities were those of ignorance more than of choice.

What set young Hooker on a course of education cannot in particular be discovered. There can be no considerable doubt, however, that the place of his preparatory training for the University was the school at Market Bosworth, established by Sir Wolstan Dixie, a wealthy Londoner having landed property at that place, and which was founded in 1586, the same year in which it is believed Hooker was born. Market Bosworth lies about twenty-five miles west from Marfield, and close to the celebrated Bosworth-field, where Henry, Earl of Richmond, defeated and killed Richard III.

The evidence on which this statement of the probable place of Hooker's early education rests, is the fact that he afterward occupied at Emmanuel College one of the two Wolstan Dixie fellowships, the conditions of which demand that the incumbent be either a relative of the founder or a graduate of Market-Bosworth School. [2] And this connection of the school with Emmanuel College may be taken also as an indication of the quality of the religious influences under which learners were there brought. For Emmanuel was distinctly a Puritan institution, and Sir Wolstan's establishment of the two fellowship foundations there, which still bear his name, must at least signify that the preparatory school he endowed would be in sympathy with the Puritan side in then existing ecclesiastical controversies. Probably the same inference may be drawn concerning the tendency of the parochial instruction imparted to the pupils in their residence at Market-Bosworth; for Rev. William Pelsant, who was rector there for more than fifty years, dying in 1634, was one of the first of the board of the school governors appointed by its founder.

It was in all likelihood while Hooker was at this school, and about a year before his going to the University, that an anxiously anticipated event occurred, which was looked for by all parties in the religious commonwealth as destined to affect profoundly the course of ecclesiastical affairs, — the death of Elizabeth, and the accession of the Scottish Presbyterian James to the English monarchy. The long reign of Elizabeth had been a protracted endeavour to maintain Conformity to the laws and ritual of the Church against Puritanism and Separatism; as the doctrines of those who desired to purify the polity and the usages of the Church, or those who desired to separate entirely from any national religious establishment whatever, were respectively called. The numbers who preferred actual divorcement from the State Church were, indeed, few compared with those who only wanted a reform of the administration and practice within it. Some distinctly Separatist movements there had been in England as early as 1566, and more important ones arose near the close of the great queen's reign; but the great body of devout objectors to the existing system of affairs were Puritans, not Separatists. And as the Puritans generally agreed with the Genevan Reformers in matters of faith, a Puritan came to stand for a man of strict morals, a Calvinist in doctrine, and a non-conformist to the rules and discipline of the Church, though not a renouncer of its fellowship or a denier of its churchly character.

Into the struggle which turmoiled nearly the whole of her reign by the conflict of the dissentient religious parties in the realm, the queen put the entire strength of her character and will. She established a High Commission Court, of which even the Romanist historian Lingard, comparing it with the Inquisition, declares, [3] "The chief difference consisted in their names." The Commission varied at different periods of its existence in its personnel and its powers; but at its ripest development, as ordered under the Great Seal in December, 1583, was composed of some forty-four bishops, privy-councillors, lawyers, and officers of State, any three of whom, under the general presidency of a bishop, constituted a court endued with full power to inquire into and punish by fine, deprivation, or imprisonment all opinions or practices different from those of the Established Church. This High Commission vindicated its character, as described by Hume, as a "real Inquisition, attended with all the iniquities as well as cruelties inseparable from that tribunal." [4] Put into effective operation by Archbishop Whitgift, in the single first year of his administration, 1584, two hundred and thirty-three ministers were suspended in six counties of Canterbury alone. [5]

Under the vigorous procedures of this body no less than a fourth part of the clergy of England were, at one time and another, under suspension; and this not on account of any moral misbehaviour or neglect of pastoral duty, but on account of conscientious convictions which prevented their wearing certain prescribed ecclesiastical vestments, their baptizing with the sign of the cross, their use of the ring in marriage, their assent to the apostolical succession of the episcopate, and their obedience to churchly regulations which were, in their opinion, unjustified by Scripture.

To people of our comfortable time some of these particulars of Puritan objection to the prescribed usages of the Church Establishment may doubtless seem insignificant; but to the actors on the then existing stage they were immensely important. The surplice was the badge of that hierarchical separation of ministry and people which long ages of ecclesiastical oppression had made offensive, and which the Puritans believed was inconsistent with the doctrine of the brotherhood of all believers in Christ. The sign of the cross in baptism was a reminder of a whole class of superstitious ceremonies which had come down from a corrupted past, in which the symbol of the crucifix was accorded a magical efficacy in exorcising evil spirits, in warding off physical dangers, as well as in securing spiritual benefits. The ring in marriage was the token of that ecclesiastical doctrine which made marriage exclusively a religious sacrament under the care and authority of the Church. The bowing at the name of Jesus was a seeming impeachment of the reverence due equally to the Father and the Spirit. The observance of saints' days brought recollections of ecclesiastical impositions which burdened life with their restrictions and bound time in fetters and obligations hard to bear. The rule of bishops associated with temporal dignities and powers seemed to the Puritan not only an assumption of unwarranted authority by one soul over another soul, but an intrusion of churchly functions into a department of things not legitimately its own. These objections were not to the participators in the then waging conflict matters of whimsey or sentiment. Every one of them stood for and represented a principle. As a national flag may be the symbol of principles central to a people's life, and of memories in which are gathered up generations of history, so to the Puritan of Elizabeth's day the ring, the cross, the surplice, were symbols of the whole of that great conflict which had been waging in England and Europe for centuries between freedom and authority, between individual conscience and established privilege.

It is impossible to conceive of any intelligent household in England, still less of any company of students even if not yet quite attained to university standing, as unconcerned in the bearing upon this great conflict of such an event as took place in 1603, when the uncouth and polemic James succeeded to the throne vacated by the strong-willed virgin queen.

All those who had in any degree sympathized with the Puritan side in the struggle, looked now for some measure of relief from the compellant hand of Conformity. The expectation was certainly not irrational. James had been brought up a Presbyterian. He had written Calvinistic commentaries on the Scriptures. He had been the ostentatious champion of the antiprelatical views of the continental reformed churches. He was a man of scholarship, and many hoped a man of Puritan convictions.

But whatever hopes of this kind were awakened were destined to early disappointment. James was met on his journey up to London from Edinburgh by a deputation of Puritan ministers, bearing what is known as the Millenary Petition from the popularly supposed thousand of its signatures. Some seven hundred and fifty of the clergy of England united in this document entitled "The humble Petition of the Ministers of the Church of England desiring Reformation of certain Ceremonies and Abuses of that Church." [6] The first specified matter needing reformation mentioned in the petition related to church services; and as it refers to what was the main issue between the Conformist and Puritan parties, it may be well to quote that portion of it here: [7]

"Namely, first, In the *'Church service,'* the *cross* in Baptism, *interrogatories* ministered to infants; *confirmations,* as superfluous, to be taken away: Baptism not to be ministered by women, and so explained: the cap and surplice not to be urged: that examination might go before the Communion: that it might be ministered with a sermon: that divers terms, *viz.* of *Priests,* and *absolution* and some other used, with the ring in marriage and other such like in the book, might be corrected: the longsomeness of suits abridged: Church songs and music moderated to better edification: that the Lord's day might not be profaned: the rest upon holy days not so strictly urged: that there might be an uniformity of doctrine prescribed: no popish opinions to be any more taught or defended: no Ministers charged to teach their people to bow at the name of Jesus: that the Canonical Scriptures be only read in the Church."

In response to this petition the king appointed a meeting at Hampton Court ostensibly to confer with representatives of the petitioners about the proposed reforms. The king nominated the disputants on both sides: those for the Establishment being nine bishops, seven deans, one archdeacon and two doctors in divinity; while the Puritans were represented by only four of their ministers, Drs. Reynolds and Sparke of Oxford, and Mr. Knewstubs and Mr. Chaderton of Cambridge. The meetings continued for three days about the middle of January, 1604, — the Puritans being admitted to audience only on the second and third, — and were, so far as any substantial result in approximating the two parties in issue, or in providing relief for conscientious dissent from the established usages of the Elizabethan settlement was concerned, an entire failure. A few minor matters of offence to the petitioners were indeed promised redress, — baptism by women and the reading of such portions of the Apocrypha as have "some repugnancy to the canonical Scripture" among them; [8] but as to the main body of the usages objected to, the king was found their defender. He put himself into the hands of the ecclesiastics, who delightedly declared, by the mouth of Whitgift, their archbishop, "undoubtedly his Majesty spoke by the especial assistance of God's Spirit." [9] He badgered the Puritan representatives with taunting questions and brow-beating lecturings; commanded them to "awaie with their snyvelings," [10] and wound up the interview with the declaration: "If this be all your party have to say, I will make them conform, or I will harry them out of the land, or else worse." [11]

The king and the bishops were mightily pleased with their part in the conference. Bancroft, falling on his knees, declared: "I protest my heart melteth for joy, that Almighty God, of his singular mercy, has given us such a king as since Christ's time has not been." [12] And James wrote to a friend in Scotland about keeping "a revel with the Puritans this two days such as was never heard the like," having "peppered them" with such arguments that they "fled from him" like schoolboys. [13]

Echoes of these events on the public stage must have reached quieter places than Market-Bosworth, whence Hooker was just taking his departure, and must have afforded topic for interested and wondering comment to duller wits than those with whom he had been there associated. Two months later found him at Cambridge and the University.

[1] Young's Massachusetts, p. 314.
[2] Cambridge Calendar; Ackermann's Cambridge, ii. 234.
[3] History of England, vol. v. chap. vi.
[4] Eliz., chap, xli.
[5] Neal, i. 157.
[6] Neal, i. 228.
[7] Strype's Whitgift, ii. 479, 480.
[8] Strype's Whitgift, ii. 501.
[9] Ibid. 498.
[10] W. Barlow, The Summe and Substance of the Conference at Hampton Court.
[11] Neal, i. 232.
[12] Ibid. 233.
[13] Strype's Whitgift, ii. 500.

Chapter Two - Education and Residence at Cambridge

When he was fellow of Emmanuel
Much learning in his solid head did dwell.

Samuel Stone: *Elegiac Verses,* 1648.

The Cambridge at which Thomas Hooker arrived in 1604, bore many traces of that Puritan influence which in this university, much more than at Oxford, had marked the history of the previous century. A very considerable number of the members of the university who after the Marian exile returned to their former or to higher posts in its service, came back with more pronounced views of nonconformity than those they carried with them abroad. At Zurich, Geneva, Frankfort, or Basel they had been received with hospitality by the continental reformers, and had come in many instances still more fully to sympathize with the theological opinions and the practices in church usage which characterized the theologians of Southwestern Germany and Switzerland. Men like the two brothers Pilkington, successively masters of St. John's College, and Roger Zelke, master of Magdalen, brought back with them from their exile an opposition to "ceremonies" as pronounced almost as that of any Separatist; an opposition which the elder Pilkington carried with him into the exercise of his bishopric of Durham when promoted thither.

But the most potent influence which had affected Cambridge emanated from Thomas Cartwright, Margaret Professor of Divinity, who preached and taught both the doctrine and polity of Geneva, and profoundly influenced the younger and rising class of fellows and scholars. Under his powerful impression the spirit of dissent from the prescribed ritual grew rapidly. Undergraduates and fellows in many of the colleges objected to the surplice, declined to kneel at the sacrament, and deemed the hierarchical orders of the ministry unscriptural. Theological degrees were denounced as being an attempt on the part of secular institutions to determine who might properly teach in religious matters.

And even when, as in the case of Dr. Whitgift, — successively Margaret and Regius Professor of Divinity, master of Trinity, and vice chancellor of the university, — no sympathy with nonconformity was found, there was often a high degree of accordancy with the continental divines in matters of theology. It was in 1595 that what are known as the Lambeth Articles — so called from the place of their subscription at the palace of that name In London, and beyond comparison the most vigorous symbol o£ Calvinism ever framed as an expression of English faith — were written by Dr. Whitaker, who succeeded Whitgift as Regius Professor of Divinity at Cambridge, and were approved by Whitgift himself, now elevated to the Archbishopric of Canterbury. The prevalent tone of teaching in the university was Calvinistic. The most celebrated preacher in Cambridge for nearly twenty years before Hooker's coming there was Rev. William Perkins, fellow of Christ College and lecturer at Great St. Andrews, a thorough Puritan in principles and a vigorous expounder of Genevan theology.

Mr. Perkins was repeatedly summoned before the High Commission on account of his irregularities in matter of ritual, and authorities are somewhat at variance as to his having been or not having been ultimately put under interdict. But at his death in 1602 the town and the university contended for the privilege of being foremost in bemoaning his loss. Into the rather warmly heated atmosphere of doctrinal and ecclesiastical controversies such as are thus indicated, young Hooker was introduced on his university entrance at about eighteen years of age. Cotton Mather says [1] that he was born "of parents that were neither unable nor unwilling to bestow upon him a liberal education." But to one acquainted with the narrow conditions of life, such as must have been lived at Marfield, it can occasion no surprise that, like many another university scholar destined to after eminence, Hooker entered college in a position implying some inferiority of pecuniary resource. He was matriculated at Queen's College as sizar, March 27, 1604; [2] a sizar at Cambridge being, like a batteller at Oxford, a student who waits upon the fellows at table, and who generally, in consideration of these and other services, is personally exempt from college charges. At some uncertain date, however, he was transferred to Emmanuel College, where he appears to have been on taking his B. A. degree in January, 1608, and his M. A. in 1611.

Occupying one of the two Wolstan Dixie fellowship foundations he remained for an indeterminable but considerable period, prosecuting his studies, and, in the latter part of the time certainly, engaging in some form of clerical work. Here then at Cambridge, as a student for certainly seven years, and as a fellow resident for some years more, Thomas Hooker was, from eighteen to probably at least twenty-eight years of age, in the focus of Puritanism, and in the midst of some of the most considerable actors in the great events of the time. How much of acquaintanceship was had among particular students of the university, it is impossible of course more than to conjecture; but it is interesting to note that there were in Cambridge during these important years of college experience several men who in the chances of after life were to be thrown more or less intimately, and some of them quite intimately, into Hooker's fellowship.

Nathaniel Ward, afterward to be minister of the gospel in Ipswich, New England, and author of the "Simple Cobbler of Agawam," had just taken his master's degree at Emmanuel in 1603, a year before Hooker entered the university, and was pursuing there his divinity studies. William Ames, with whom Hooker was subsequently to be joined in the care of the church of exiles in Rotterdam, and in the publication of Ames's book against Ceremonies, a graduate of Christ College, was resident in Cambridge nearly all the time till Hooker became a fellow at Emmanuel, and was already challenged by the authorities for his outspokenness against church vestments, and his public denunciation of games countenanced by the clergy. Peter Bulkley, afterward to be associated with Hooker in the moderatorship of more than one historic New England assembly, and pastor of the church in Concord, was taking his M. A. at St. John's College in 1605, a year after Hooker's arrival at Cambridge. John Cotton, a year older than Hooker, and a student of earlier start in letters, who was to sail in the same vessel with him across the seas, and to be to Massachusetts what Hooker was to Connecticut, reached his B. A. at Emmanuel a year before Hooker was matriculated, and arrived at his M. A. in 1606. Francis Higginson, Hooker's junior by a year, who was to precede both him and Cotton in the American enterprise, attained his B. A. at Jesus College a year later, and his M. A. two years later, than Hooker's arrival at the same standing. John Wilson, Hooker's junior by two years, and afterward so long Cotton's associate in the pastorate of the Boston church, entered Kings College in 1602, and after pursuing the usual university course, and attempting awhile the study of law, returned in 1610 to Cambridge to put himself under the special instruction of Mr. Ames, and to prosecute his studies in divinity.

All these and several other afterward distinguished men who were to be in one way or another closely associated with Hooker in his subsequent history, were in Cambridge during some part of his residence there; and with them all it was quite possible, and with several of them altogether probable, that he had personal acquaintance.

The particular college with which Thomas Hooker was most identified — Emmanuel — and where he held one of the Wolstan Dixie fellowships, was, from its foundation, regarded as a Puritan institution. It was established in 1584 by a charter granted by Elizabeth to Sir Walter Mildmay, a prominent statesman and councillor in the service of that sovereign, and employed by her in many responsible trusts. There is nothing in the charter of the institution to suggest any deviation from the established order, but rumours of its founder's intention to encourage dissent were early promulgated; and the queen, on his coming to court soon after the allowance of the new institution, is said to have addressed him: "Sir Walter, I hear you have erected a Puritan foundation;" to which he is said to have made reply, "No, madam, far be it from me to countenance anything contrary to your established laws; but I have set an acorn which, when it becomes an oak, God alone knows what will be the fruit thereof." [3] Something of the diplomatist is probably discoverable in this reply, especially as Sir Walter conditioned his foundation of the college upon the acceptance by Laurence Chaderton of the mastership. Chaderton had always the reputation of belonging to the Puritan side in the then current controversies. As such he was chosen by James as one of the four ministers to represent the Puritan cause in the famous mock conference at Hampton Court a few years later; on which occasion he is said to have fallen on his knees and entreated the railing king that the "wearing of the *surplis* and the vse of the *Crosse in Baptisme* might not be vrged vpō some honest, godly, and painfull ministers in some partes of *Lancashire.*" [4] A pious and learned man, he was one of the translators of the new version of the Bible authorized by James; the section on which he with his immediate co-labourers was employed being "from Chronicles to Canticles, inclusive." [5] Chaderton lived to be one hundred and three years old; and though he is spoken of as a "moderate" man in his spirit, he had fire enough in his bones in 1622, at eighty-six years of age, to resign the mastership of Emmanuel in favour of the celebrated Calvinistic preacher John Preston, fearing that otherwise an Arminian successor might be chosen.

And it must be confessed that Emmanuel College under his and Mr. Preston's guidance vindicated the character given to it by Carter at a somewhat later date than Chaderton's day, as "neither more nor less than a mere nursery of Puritans." [6] During the Commonwealth no less than eleven masters of other colleges in Cambridge were graduates of Emmanuel, all more or less distinct representatives of Puritan views.

A single but very significant hint of the temper of things in Emmanuel remains to this day. Alone of all the college chapels in Cambridge or Oxford, its original chapel — now, indeed, disused for this service, and employed as the library — stands, as built by Sir Walter, facing north and south instead of east and west. A report made to Archbishop Laud in 1633 of the condition of affairs at the college, probably gives a substantially accurate account of matters as they were twenty years before, when Hooker occupied a fellowship there. The reporter says: —

"In Emmanuel College their chappel is not consecrate. At Surplice prayers they sing nothing but certain riming Psalms of their own appointment instead of ye Hymmes between ye Lessons. And at Lessons they read not after ye order appointed in ye Callendar, but after another continued course of their own. All Service is there done and performed by the Minister alone. When they preach or Commonplace they omit all service after ye first or second Lesson at ye furthest." [7]

Indeed, the vigour of Emmanuel's Puritanism was a popular proverb. The doggerel and ridiculing lines of the "Mad Puritan" in Percy's Ballads have all their significance from the recognized character of the college to which they refer: —

"In the house of pure Emmanuel
I had my education;
Where, my friends surmise,
I dazzled my eyes
With the light of Revelation.

"Boldly I preach,
Hate a cross and a surplice;
Mitres, copes, and rochets;
Come hear me pray,
Nine times a day,
And fill your head with crotchets."

The avowed design of Sir Walter Mildmay in establishing a new college was to train up a "godly ministry;" and however wise or unwise minor features of the administration may have been, tried by the test of its avowed intention Emmanuel was certainly a success. The acorn planted only in 1584, which before Cromwell's time had fruited with such names — not to mention any already spoken of: — as William Bradshaw, Ralph Cudworth, John Richardson, John Harvard, William Eyre, Jeremiah Burroughs, Ephraim Udal, Richard Holdsworth, Thomas Shepard, Samuel Hudson, Thomas Hill, Nathaniel Rogers, Stephen Marshall, Samuel Stone, Anthony Burgess, William Bridge, Anthony Tuckney, and Bishop Hall, among many others nearly or equally distinguished, must surely be regarded as an acorn well worth planting.

Of Hooker's personal experiences during the years of his residence in Cambridge scanty authentic memorials remain. These years themselves were marked by some events on the public stage which must have been felt at Cambridge quite as sensibly as anywhere else. It was in his second year's residence that the plot to blow up the king and Parliament in the interest of the Romanist party, by Catesby, Digby, Guy Fawkes, and others, was discovered just in time to have no worse consequences than the execution of the conspirators. It was just when he was taking his B. A., in 1608, that John Robinson and his Scrooby church, unable to find toleration for Independency in England, sought refuge and liberty in Holland. Two years later, James, the whilom Presbyterian of Scotland, forced Episcopacy into the country north of the Tweed.

It was just as Hooker was taking his M. A., in 1611, that James inaugurated the protracted fight of the Stuarts with the Commons of England by dissolving his first Parliament. The years following, to 1620, saw the clouds of civil and religious trouble steadily deepening. They beheld the scandals of Somerset's elevation to power, of Overbury's murder, of the sale of peerages for money payments, of the dismissal of Lord Coke, of the rise to supremacy of the ignorant but dangerous Buckingham. They saw the peremptory dissolution of James's second Parliament, the negotiations for the marriage of Prince Charles with the Infanta of Spain, the execution of Sir Walter Raleigh, the outbreak in Europe of the Thirty Years' War, — a struggle virtually between Protestantism and Romanism, — and perhaps least noticed of all, the planting of Plymouth Colony in America by English exiles for the sake of religious liberty. These things, and matters involved in them, could not but have been things of interest, and some of them of intense concern, to the nearly three thousand students of the various colleges of the university.

But to Hooker himself an event which occurred apparently after his reception of his master's degree and during his residence as Dixie fellow, was of greater personal moment than any yet alluded to. This event, to use phrases which he was accustomed to employ in characterizing similar experiences in others, was his Effectual Calling, and Implantation into Christ. Whatever may have hitherto been his religious convictions or feelings, this was the period of that great spiritual crisis which he would have called his conversion.

That his processes of mind in this passage of his inward history should have been sombre and tumultuous might easily be anticipated. Such was the common course of religious experience in his time. And there is reason to believe that it was unusually common at Cambridge, where the strenuous presentation of some of the sterner features of the Calvinistic system, by powerful popular preachers like Perkins, Baynes, and Gibbs, had given a kind of established direction to the courses of men's experience under the operation of strong religious emotions. But there was also something in Mr. Hooker's temperament, and probably something also, as we shall have occasion hereafter to see, in his theological views and tendencies, to make this religious struggle in his own case unusually protracted and severe. He is said [8] to have long afterward observed of this passage of his experience, "that in the time of his agonies, he could reason himself to the rule, and conclude that there was no way but submission to God, and lying at the foot of his mercy in Christ Jesus, and waiting humbly there till he should please to perswade the soul of his favour; nevertheless, when he came to apply this rule unto himself, in his own condition, his reasoning would fail him, he was able to do nothing." Readers of his treatise on the "Soules Humiliation" will not wonder why he found it hard to apply his "rule" to his own case, or why his reasoning failed him. The extreme conceptions of what is involved in a true submission of the soul to God set forth in that treatise, and to some extent in other of Mr. Hooker's writings, have always, whenever presented, been a source of perplexity to men. As expounded a hundred and fifty years later in the writings of Samuel Hopkins, they not only introduced an era of controversy in theological debate, but a period of bewilderment and trouble in the individual religious experience of multitudes. The making a willingness to be lost a condition precedent to a reasonable hope of being saved, whether prescribed by Hooker or his son-in-Jaw Shepard, or by the celebrated Newport divine who has in New England theology given his name to the particular dogma in question, is and must ever be a prescription perplexing and embarrassing to the process of most people's religious experience.

How far this particular notion of what is necessary before a soul can rest in a cheerful hope of God's mercy actually embarrassed the process of attaining that quietude in Hooker's own case, it is probably impossible to say; but his doubts and perturbations were protracted. He is said [9] to have remarked, "I can compare with any man living for fears." And it is not without a touch of pathos that it is recorded [10] that one considerable source of relief to him in this time of trouble came from the young sizar who waited upon him, whose "prudent and piteous carriage" and "discreet and proper compassions" were of "singular help." The giver of this important aid was Mr. Simeon Ashe, afterward a graduate of Emmanuel, a minister in Staffordshire, chaplain to the Earl of Warwick in the civil wars, rector of St. Austin in London for twenty years, and though, as Calamy says, "a nonconformist of the old stamp," one of the divines who went to Breda to meet Charles H. just before his restoration. The piety and moderation of which the general course of this Puritan minister's history was an illustration, had apparently one of its earlier and most useful manifestations in helping to lead the Fellow whom it was his function to serve into a more cheerful assurance of religious welfare.

There appears to be evidence that after passing this crisis-point in his religious history, Mr. Hooker continued a considerable time in the university as catechist and lecturer. Here and in the vicinity he began the systematic development into sermonic form of those essays on experimental religion which constituted always the main bulk of his preaching, and over the general track of which he seems again and again to have gone, at Cambridge, at Chelmsford, and in his successive ministries in Holland and America. These sermons, which are in effect a kind of body of divinity, not so much of the doctrinal as of the experimental kind, were immensely popular. They grew out of, and were exactly suited to, the religious feeling of the period. They gave their author an immediate and wide distinction as a powerful applier of the gospel to men's hearts and consciences. They were circulated to some extent in copies enlarged from shorthand notes surreptitiously taken. They were collected with less or more accuracy into volumes published not always with their author's knowledge or sanction. And they make up in the whole that body of writing about the general subject of the application of religion to the soul, which as one substantially connected treatise, though divided in title into various subordinate portions, there will be occasion hereafter more particularly, though briefly, to notice.

[1] Magnalia (ed. 1820, i. 303)
[2] Records of the College, and letters of librarians of that institution and Emmanuel.
[3] Cooper's Annals of Cambridge, ii. 354.
[4] Barlow's Summe and Substance, p. 99.
[5] Ackermann's Cambridge, ii. 237.
[6] Ackermann's Cambridge, ii. 228.
[7] Cooper's Annals of Cambridge, ii. 383.
[8] Magnalia, i. 303.
[9] Magnalia, i. 314.
[10] Ibid. 303.

Chapter Three - Hooker's English Ministry

His knowledge in Theologie Divine,
In Chelmsford *Lectures divers years did shine.*

Samuel Stone: *Elegiac Verses.*

Leaving out of view the functions which Mr. Hooker may have performed as catechist and lecturer while still resident at Cambridge, the probable period of his exercise of ministerial duty in England was ten or twelve years, — that is to say, from 1618 or 1620 to his flight to Holland in 1630. This space of time was all included in the duration of the archbishopric of George Abbot, who had been appointed to the primacy on the death of Bancroft in 1610. These twenty-two years of Abbot's nominal headship of the Church of England, and especially the last thirteen of them which cover the period of Hooker's English ministry, were momentous years in Puritan story. Abbot himself was a Calvinist, and by conviction attached to the cause of Puritanism and the Parliament. He advocated a definite policy of Protestantism abroad, and it was his influence which sent English representatives to the Synod of Dort in 1618-19. He favoured the maintenance of the Puritan Lectureships, which had become so extended a part of the machinery employed for the dissemination of the principles of which nonconformity stood the representative. By his doctrinal sympathies with his pragmatic sovereign and by his official place as head of the hierarchy, he seemed to stand in a favourable position for mediating between the contending parties in the civil and religious commonwealths. But Abbot had no skill as a reconciler; events were too strong for him, perhaps were too strong for any one. The years of his primacy saw the progressively definite identification of Puritanism with the Parliament, of prerogative with churchly authority. The Presbyterian king put himself increasingly into the hands of Arminian prelacy; the Commons more and more accepted the leadership of Calvinistic nonconformity.

The great figure on the stage of this generation of English story, and the great power by which this definition of party lines was effected, was William Laud. Laud had been from his university days a rival and opponent of the archbishop; and during all the later years of Abbot's nominal headship of the establishment it was far more the inferior than the superior church-functionary who gave direction to the course of religious affairs, and influenced the counsels of his sovereign. Laud's advancement was rapid, and indicative alike of his personal abilities and of the growing conviction on the part of the king, which he formulated in the characteristic saying, "Presbyterianism agreeth as well with monarchy as God and the devil." In 1611 Laud was appointed president of St. John's College, Oxford. The same year made him also chaplain to the king. The year 1616 saw him Dean of Gloucester; in 1621 he was Bishop of St. David's; in 1626, of Bath and Wells; in 1628, of the important See of London. He guided, almost regulated, the church patronage by giving the king a list of the clergy, marked for advancement or neglect by the cabalistic sign "O" or "P" (Orthodox or Puritan) affixed to their names. His hand, as there will be occasion to see, was in every considerable event of the period covered by our Hooker's English ministry.

This ministry began in Mr. Hooker's appointment, probably some time between 1618 and 1620, to the rectorship of the little parish of Esher in Surrey, a small place sixteen miles southwest from the Parliament houses in London.

That Mr. Hooker's principles allowed him to go there was owing to the fact that the living was a donative one, — given, that is to say, directly by the patron of the benefice, a Mr. Francis Drake, and not requiring presentation to the bishop and induction by his order; to which presentation Mr. Hooker's nonconforming views would not allow him to accede, and which would therefore have availed to exclude him from the greater part of the benefices in England. Esher [1] was and is a pleasant, small village, built on a rising ground a little distance from the Thames, and includes in its parochial boundaries two or three ancient manorial properties, one of which, Esher Place, was occupied by Cardinal Wolsey after his disgrace; another, Clermont, was formerly the home of Lord Clive; then of Princess Charlotte, and now of the widow of Prince Leopold. Adjoining Esher Common is the tract of ground which used to be known as Sandon Farm, now the scene of the Sandon races.

That Esher was, and is still, a little village with so much that is picturesque in its situation and convenient in its proximity to the city, the rector at present (1891) incumbent ascribes to the fact of its being hemmed in and limited by these large landed estates.

The church where Mr. Hooker preached still stands, though not at present used for public worship. It is very small, with a nave and chancel only, except that at a period considerably later than that we are now speaking of, the Duke of Newcastle, who occupied Clermont before Lord Clive, built a kind of chamber room or gallery on one side of it. The glass of the chancel windows is said once to have been fine, but no vestige of its former glories remains. At the west end the nave is surmounted by a low pyramidal tower in which formerly hung three bells, one of which was understood to be a war-trophy brought by Sir Francis Drake from St. Domingo. The living was worth only forty pounds a year; the place of worship not capable of stretching beyond a hundred sittings; the congregation a few lowly people of the village, and members of the manor house families.

The patron of the living, a gentleman of the same name, and a kinsman of the great admiral, received the rector into his house, and gave him a home in his family, — a fact attended with important consequences to the rector.

The persuasive cause of the procuring of Mr. Hooker's services at Esher was the condition of Mr. Drake's wife. The story is told in a little volume printed the year Mr. Hooker died. It bears the characteristically quaint title of the time, "Trodden down Strength by the God of Strength, or Mrs. Drake Revived, showing her strange and rare Case, great and manifold afflictions for tenne years together. Related by her friend Hart On-hi. London, 1647." Mrs. Drake was an invalid and hypochondriac. She had already worn out the consolations of two worthy ministers — Rev. Mr. Dod, the author of a commentary on the Decalogue, and hence popularly known as Decalogue Dod; and Rev. Mr. Usher, afterward Primate of Ireland — in their efforts to persuade her that she had not committed the unpardonable sin.

Mr. Dod being obliged to leave her after three years' wrestling with her case, tidings came to Mr. Drake of one Mr. Hooker, then at Cambridge, now in New England: A great Scholar, an acute Disputant, a strong learned, a wise modest man, every way rarely qualified; who being a Non-conformitan in judgement, not willing to trouble himself with *Presentative* Livings, was contented and persuaded by Mr. Dod to accept of that poor Living of 40l. per annum: This worthy man accepted of the place, having withal his dyet and lodging at Esher, Mr. Drake's house."

Mr. Hooker's ministrations seem to have been useful. "For Mr. Hooker being newly come from the University had a new answering methode (though the same thing) wherewith shee was marvellously delighted." Just how long or precisely at what date these ministrations were rendered is not stated, but the period came when Mrs. Drake felt "that her time on earth was but of small continuance. About which time it fell out that Mr. Hooker also having acted his part with her, and done his best, to comfort, uphold and rectifie her spirit, ... by God's providence he was married unto her waiting-woman: After which both of them having lived some time after with her, and he cal'd to be Lecturer at Chelmsford in Essex, they both left her."

It is pleasant to be assured that the counsels of Mr. Hooker, and of Mr. Dod which were again renewed, did much to help Mrs. Drake, and that she was "more cheerful in mind divers years," coming indeed to her end at last in "a Fit of sudden, extream, ravishing, unsupportable Joy, beyond the Strength of Mortality to retain, or be long capable of, ...which put Mr. Dod, her Husband, and all of them to a *non-plus*, as being beyond all Experience; they in all their lifetime never having seen or heard of the like."

The chief recorded result to Mr. Hooker himself, however, of this Esher experience was his marrying Mrs. Drake's waiting-woman, Susanna. Who this young woman was, whose future was to be so full of vicissitude, who was to be exiled to Holland, to voyage the Atlantic, to be carried on a litter through the Massachusetts forests to Connecticut, to survive her husband we know not how long, and to be buried we know not where — there seems no way at present to determine.

That she was esteemed in Mr. Drake's family is evidenced by the provision in Mr. Drake's will, dated March 13, 1634, by which he gave to "Johana Hooker whoe is now in New England £30 to be paid her the day of her marriage." This was Mr. Hooker's daughter who married Rev, Thomas Shepard, and from a comparison of dates would seem to have been his oldest child, and may have been born at Esher, and named Joanna for Mrs. Drake, whose maiden name was Joanna Tothill.

Esher's proximity to London favoured the more ready recognition of Mr. Hooker's gifts as a preacher, and it appears that some ineffectual attempts were made to secure his establishment in some capacity at Colchester in Essex, "whereto Mr. Hooker did very much incline, ...but the providence of God gave an obstruction to that settlement."

Mather says [2] Hooker's desire to be at Colchester was on account of its proximity to Mr. Rogers of Dedham, whom he used to call "the prince of all the preachers in England;" but "it was an observation which Mr. Hooker would sometimes afterwards use unto his friends 'that the providence of God often diverted him from employment in such places as he himself desired, and still directed him to such places as he had no thoughts of.'"

But sometime probably in 1626 an invitation was extended and accepted for Mr. Hooker's establishment as Lecturer in connection with the church of St. Mary at Chelmsford, Essex, then under the rectoral care of Rev. John Michaelson. Possibly he had been resident a little while previous in the immediate vicinity., for the parish register of Great Baddow contains the following entry: "Anne, daughter of Mr. Thomas Hooker, clerk, and Susan his wife, baptized at Great Baddow, Essex, January 5. 1626." As pertinent to Mr. Hooker's family relationships it may also here as appropriately as anywhere be remarked that the Chelmsford parish register contains the record, under date of April 9, 1628, of the baptism of "Sarah daughter of Mr. Thomas Hooker and Susan his wife;" and on August 26, 1629, of her burial.

Chelmsford was a busy town twenty-nine miles east from London, and its old Gothic church is an edifice of great antiquity. The great-tower and most of the older portions of the building are made of the flint nodules, from the size of the fist upward, found in the chalk-pits of the neighbourhood, laid in cement. The arch of the Norman door in the great-tower has the Boar and Mullet of the De Vere family. In 1641 the Parliamentary visitation was the occasion of a riot in which the beautiful glass windows were destroyed, and Rev. Dr. Michaelson, the rector, subjected to personal indignities and injury. The roof of the nave fell in, in 1800, and the repair in other stone than that which characterizes the older portion of the structure has an unpleasing and incongruous appearance. The patronage of the church was given or sold by Henry VHI. to Roger Mildmay, ancestor of Sir Roger Mildmay, founder of Emmanuel College; and twenty generations of the family sleep underneath its roof. This noble old sanctuary became for between three and four years the scene of Mr. Hooker's public labours as Lecturer.

These Lectureships, to which reference has already several times been made, were one of the most characteristic outgrowths of the Puritan movement in England. They were designed to secure a more efficient preaching service than could be often had from the legal incumbent of a benefice. They were generally supported by voluntary gifts of wealthy Puritans, though sometimes endowed by permanent funds; and were customarily held by persons having scruples about the ceremonies and the vestments, and consequently not always, though generally, in priest's orders. The Lecturer preached on market-days and Sunday afternoons, as supplemental to the regularly appointed church services. The system was immensely popular with the multitude, who were dissatisfied with "no preaching and dumb ministers," as those who confined themselves to the liturgy were called, and developed into wide and large proportions in the country generally.

But by so much as Lectureships were popular with the masses they were obnoxious to the church party, who sympathized with Laud and with the intensifying demand for Conformity represented by the king. Already, some four years previous to Hooker's entering on his Chelmsford Lectureship, James, in 1622, had issued injunctions to the clergy, through the archbishop, forbidding any one of them under the standing of "a bishop or dean [to] presume to preach in any popular auditory on the deep points of predestination, election, reprobation, or of the universality, efficacy, resistibility, or irresistibility of God's grace;" and prescribing that all Sunday afternoon sermons be rigidly restricted to exposition of the "Catechism, Creed, or Ten Commandments." [3] This was a direct stroke at the Lecturers. The Puritan revival had brought these doctrinal topics to the forefront of debate, and these themes were now prohibited. Charles followed up his father's attempt to silence the Lecturers by his proclamation in June, 1626, — just about the time Hooker was making his first essays at Chelmsford, — forbidding discussion of any opinions not justified by the "literal and grammatical sense" [4] of the Articles of the Church. Lecturers were ordered to read the service of the liturgy before the delivery of the homily, and to wear the surplice in doing so.

It was under the at least nominal imposition of these limitations that all Lecturers were placed during the period which followed Hooker's arrival at Chelmsford. Doubtless these limitations were often disregarded. Certainly he disregarded most of them. Probably he preached in the Genevan gown rather than the surplice. Certainly he treated of election, reprobation, the resistibility or irresistibility of God's grace without mincing. His published sermons — the fruit, as has been said, of his repeated traversing of experimental points of divinity at Cambridge, Esher, and Chelmsford — leave no doubt on that point.

Nor is there any doubt of the wide and profound impression made by his discourses. Auditors flocked to his ministrations from great distances, and "some of great quality among the rest," [5] — one of whom was the Earl of Warwick, who afterward sheltered and befriended the Lecturer's family when Mr. Hooker was forced to flee the country. His labours resulted not only in the visible reformation of morals in Chelmsford, but in stimulating to similar endeavours many other ministers of the surrounding region.

It was probably of this period of his English ministry that the occurrences took place which Mather narrates concerning the effect of Mr. Hooker's preaching, which may as well be given in Mather's language: [6]

"A profane person designing therein only an ungodly diversion and merriment said unto his companions, *Come, let us go hear what that bawling* Hooker *will say to us;* and thereupon with an intention to make sport, unto *Chelmsford* lecture they came. The man had not been long in the church, before the *quick and powerful word* of God in the mouth of his faithful *Hooker,* pierced the soul of him; he came out with an awakened and a distressed soul, and by the further blessing of God upon Mr. *Hooker's* ministry he arrived unto a true *conversion;* for which cause he would not afterwards leave that blessed ministry, but went a *thousand leagues* to attend it, and enjoy it. Another memorable thing of this kind was this; it was Mr. *Hooker's* manner once' a year to visit his native county; and in one of these visits he had an invitation to preach in the great church of *Leicester.* One of the chief burgesses in the town much opposed his preaching there; and when he could not prevail to hinder it, he set certain *fidlers* at work to disturb him in the church-porch, or church-yard. But such was the vivacity of Mr. *Hooker,* as to proceed in what he was about, without either the damping of his mind, or the drowning of his *voice;* whereupon the man himself went unto the church-door to over-hear what he said. It pleased God so to accompany some words uttered by Mr. *Hooker,* as thereby to procure, first the *attention* and then the *conviction* of that wretched man; who then came to Mr. *Hooker* with a penitent confession of his wickedness, and became indeed so penitent a convert, as to be at length a sincere *professor* and *practiser* of the godliness, whereof he had been a *persecutor.*"

Of the same date is also another of Mather's stories [7] concerning Mr. Hooker's preaching at Chelmsford on the occasion of "a fast kept throughout the nation," when —

"Mr. *Hooker* then, in the presence of the Judges, and before a vast congregation, declared freely the sins of *England,* and the plagues that would come for such sins; and in his prayer he besought the God of heaven to set on the heart of the King what his own mouth had spoken, and in the second chapter of *Malachy,* and the eleventh and twelfth verses (in his prayer he so distinctly quoted it!) *An abomination is committed, Judah hath married the daughter of a strange God, the Lord will cut off the man that doeth this.* Though the Judges turned unto the place thus quoted, yet Mr. *Hooker* came into no trouble; but it was [not?] long before the kingdom did."

It is in connection with this incident of more than indirectly passing censure on the king before the judges, that Mather quotes a saying of one that had "observed the heroical spirit and courage with which this great man fulfilled his ministry," that *"He was a person who while doing his master's work. would put a king in his pocket."*

Meantime, however, the tension between the king and Parliament was growing hourly more severe. In the middle of July, 1628, Laud had been transferred to the See of London, and henceforth had the ear of the king in all matters. The Parliament, which met on the 20th of January, 1629, proceeded at once to the discussion of the religious question; and on the 25th of February certain *Heads of Articles* were presented by the Commons, complaining of the "subtle and pernicious spreading of the Arminian faction;" of the "bold and unwarrantable" introduction of "sundry new ceremonies" and "bringing men into question and trouble for not obeying that for which there is no authority." The king rejoined by dissolving Parliament. For eleven years there was not to be another. Government was now in the hands of prerogative only.

The decks cleared for action, Laud now turned attention to the Lecturers. Long hateful to him, he now presented a series of *Considerations* to the king for their regulation or suppression. He alleged that the Lecturers were "the people's creatures," and "blew the bellows of their sedition." He inveighed against "Emmanuel and Sidney Colleges" as "nurseries of Puritanism," and implored that "grave and orthodox men" be appointed governors therein.

The king, nothing loath, authorized the promulgation of "certain Orders to be observed and put in execution by the several Bishops." [8] Among these orders were the following: "That in all parishes the afternoon service be turned into catechising by question and answer;" "that every lecturer read Divine service before lectures in surplice and hood;" that lecturers "preach in gowns, and not in cloaks, as too many do use;" and that in general the former instructions concerning the avoidance of matters connected with the predestinarian controversy be strictly observed.

Armed with these newly sharpened weapons, the bishop proceeded to clear his diocese of the obnoxious blowers of the bellows of sedition. Among those who this year were silenced for nonconformity to the orders of the bishop, in the near vicinity of Chelmsford, were John Rogers of Dedham, Daniel Rogers of Wethersfield, and John Archer of Halsted. [9] The blow fell also on Mr. Hooker. How likely it was to do so appears vividly set forth in a letter written by Rev. Samuel Collins, Vicar of Braintree, in a letter to Dr. Duck, Laud's Chancellor, which under date of May 20, 1629, obviously recognizes the commencement of ecclesiastical procedures already against the Chelmsford Lecturer. Mr. Collins writes: [10] —

"Since my return from London I have spoken with Mr. Hooker, but I have small hope of prevailing with him. All the favour he desires is that my Lord of London would not bring him into the High Commission Court, but permit him quietly to depart out of the diocese...All men's eares are now filled with ye obstreperous clamours of his followers against my Lord ... as a man endeavouring to suppress good preaching and advance Popery. All would be here very calme and quiet if he might depart. ... If he be suspended its the resolution of his friend and himself to settle his abode in Essex, and maintenance is promised him in plentifull manner for the fruition of his private conference, which hath already more impeached the peace of our church than his pub. lique ministry. His genius will still haunte all the pulpits in ye country, where any of his scholers may be admitted to preach...There be divers young ministers about us...that spend their time in conference with him; and return home and preach what he hath brewed....Our people's pallats grow so out of tast, ye noe food contents them but of Mr. Hooker's dressing. I have lived in Essex to see many changes, and have scene the people idolizing many new ministers and lecturers, but this man surpasses them all for learning and some other considerable partes and...gains more and far greater followers than all before him. ...If my Lord tender his owne future peace ... let him connive at Mr. Hooker's departure."

Apparently Dr. Duck was inclined to the same view; for, probably at the chancellor's instance, Mr. Collins reported, on June 3, an attempt to confer with Mr. Hooker on the subject: [11] —

"On Monday I rode to Chelmsford to speake with him, but found him gone...and purposed to returne to London to appeare before my Lord upon the first day of this terme, at which time I cannot be at London ... I pray God direct my Lord of London in this weighty business...this will prove a leading case, and the issue thereof will either much incourage or else discourage the regular clergie. All men's heads, tongues, eyes, and ears are in London, and all the counties about London, taken up with plotting, talking, and expecting what will be the conclusion of Mr. Hooker's business. ... It drowns the noise of the greate question of Tonnage and Poundage. I dare not say halfe of that I heare; paper walls are easily broken open. But hearing and knowing as much as I doe, I dare be bold to say that if he be once quietly gone, my Lord hath overcame the greatest difficulty in governing this parte of his diocese ... let him be as cautelous as he will, yet in his present course the humour of our people will undoe him."

Apparently, however, Mr. Hooker carried out his purpose of appearing at London before the bishop, and a bond was taken of a Mr. Nash of Much Waltham in the sum of £50 for his appearance when called for.

But on the 3d of November following, renewed complaint was made to Laud of Hooker's continuance in "his former practices;" the rector of Rawreth, one Rev. John Browning, who presented the complaint, entreating that it may "please your lordship to grant us ye helpe of your honourable authority, if not to ye suppressinge and casting out (as we hope) such an one from amongst us, yet at least to the defendinge us who live in obedience."

Stirred up probably by tidings of this communication, the following petition to the bishop was drawn up under date of Nov. 10, 1629, and signed by forty -nine ministers of the vicinage, and forwarded to Laud, asking a stay of adverse proceedings: [12] —

"Whereas we have heard that your honour hath been informed against Mr. Thomas Hooker, preacher at Chelmsford, that the conformable ministers of these partes desire his removal from the place, we, whose names are here under written, being ministers of the partes adjoining, all beneficed men, and obedient to His Majesty's ecclesiastical laws, doe humbly give your lordship to understand that we all esteeme and knowe the said Mr. Thomas Hooker to be, for doctryne, orthodox, and life and conversation honest, and for his disposition peaceable, no wayes turbulent or factious, and so not doubting but he will contynue that good course, commending him and his lawfull suite to your lordship's honourable favour, ... we humbly take our leave, and remaine your honour's humbly at command."

Samuel Collins, Duck's correspondent, John Michaelson the Chelmsford rector, and Stephen Marshall, the afterward celebrated member of the Westminster Assembly of divines, were among the signers of this petition.

Seven days later, what was in effect a counter-petition, signed by forty-one of the Essex ministers, — two of whom had signed also the previous petition, — was forwarded to Laud, praying the bishop "not [to] relax unto us that tye by which we stand obliged to the lawful ceremonies of our church, yet to enforce these irregulars to conforme with us. That soe there may effectually be wrought a generall uniformitie amongst us all." [13]

The second petition was much more to Laud's mind than the first; and it must have been almost immediately after it that Mr. Hooker was compelled to lay down his lectureship at Chelmsford and to retire to Little Baddow, a small hamlet about four miles away, where, "at the request of several eminent persons, he kept a school in *his own hired house.*" [14] It was probably in connection with this demission of his ministry that he preached a sermon which some eleven or twelve years afterward, in 1641, got into print, entitled "The Danger of Desertion, or a Farwell Sermon of Mr. *Thomas Hooker,* Sometimes Minister of God's Word at *Chainsford* in *Essex;* but now of *New* England."

The theme of the discourse is the peril of England in the threatened withdrawal of God's favour, whereof the preacher indicated that he saw manifest tokens. The sermon bears marks of haste and heat in the delivery, and was probably printed from imperfect notes, and does not convey the best impression of the preacher's style. It has, however, occasional touches of his vivid use of common illustrations; as where he says, [15] —

"We may take up the complaint of the Prophet, Isa. 64. 7. *No man stirs tip himselfe to lay hold upon God:* For this is our misery, if that we have quietnesse and commodity we are well enough, thus we play mock-holy-day with God, the Gospell we make it our pack-horse: God is going, his glory is departing, England hath seene her best dayes, and now evill dayes are befalling us: God is packing up his Gospell, because no body will buy his wares, nor come to his price. Oh lay hands on God! and let him not goe out of your coasts, he is a going, stop him, and let not thy God depart, lay siege against him with humble and hearty closing with him, suffer him not to say, as if that he were going, farewell, or fare ill England, God hath said that he will doe this, and because that he hath said it, he will doe it, therefore prepare to meet thy God, O England!"

Or again: [16] —

"Thou *England* which wast lifted up to heaven with meanes shall be abased and brought downe to hell; for if the mighty works which have been done in thee had been done in India or Turky, they would have repented ere this; therefore *Capernaums* place is *Englands* place, which is the most insufferablest torment of all; and marke what I say, the poore native Turks and Infidels shall have a cooler summer parlour in hell then you; for we stand at a high rate, we were highly exalted, therefore shall our torments be the more to beare."

Mr. Hooker's employment as teacher at Little Baddow cannot have been of long duration, and is chiefly memorable for the association with him there of John Eliot, who says, [17] —

"To this place I was called through the infinite riches of God's mercy in Christ

Jesus to my poor soul: for here the Lord said unto my dead soul, *live;* and through the grace of Christ I do live, and I shall live for ever! When I came to this blessed family, I then saw, and never before, the power of godliness in its lively vigour and efficacy."

But Laud had not forgotten the Chelmsford Lecturer in the Little Baddow schoolmaster. He was cited, on the 10th of July, 1630, to appear before the High Commission Court. This time he did not respond. His bondsman, Mr. Nash, a tenant of the Earl of Warwick, being reimbursed by Mr. Hooker's Chelmsford friends, paid the penal sum into the court j the Earl meanwhile providing for Mr. Hooker's family at a place called Old Park, while he himself got secretly aboard a vessel for Holland. It was doubtless well that he fled. The experience of Alexander Leighton, another nonconformist minister, who was this year pilloried, whipped, branded, slit in the nostrils, and deprived by successive mutilation of his ears, might have been, at least in part, his experience.

His pursuers arrived at the seaside just too late for his arrest. Cotton Mather narrates [18] several characteristic "remarkables" in connection with his flight, — as the wind shifting in his favour, which had been contrary, as soon as he got aboard; and his standing forth, like Paul, when the vessel ran aground and was in "eminent hazard of *shipwrack* upon a shelf of sand," assuring the sailors that they should all be preserved. Certain it is they landed safely in Holland.

[1] Manning's History and Antiquities of Surrey, vol. ii.: art. "Esher."
[2] Magnalia, i. 304.
[3] Neal, i. 272.
[4] Ibid. 201.
[5] Magnalia, i. 304.
[6] Ibid. i. 306, 307.
[7] Magnalia, i. 313.
[8] Neal, i. 298.
[9] David's Nonconformity in Essex, p. 146.
[10] Ibid. 150, 1 51.
[11] David's Nonconformity in Essex, p. 151-152.
[12] David's Nonconformity in Essex, p. 153.
[13] David's Nonconformity in Essex, p. 158.
[14] Magnalia, i. 305.
[15] Page 15.
[16] Page 20.
[17] Magnalia, i. 305.
[18] Magnalia, i. 307.

Chapter Four - Life in Holland and Departure for America

Now I live, if you stand fast in the Lord.

Salutation to the Church at Newtown: *Magnalia,* i. 310.

Arrived in Holland, Mr. Hooker was for a period of uncertain duration resident at Amsterdam; and negotiations looking to his association in the pastorate of the British Presbyterian Church there, then under the care of Rev. John Paget, were begun. This church, founded in 1607, was ecclesiastically in fellowship with the Dutch establishment, received provision from the State, and had assigned to it a deserted chapel of the Beguyn nuns for its place of worship. [1] Mr. Paget had been identified with the church from the founding of it, and had perhaps something of the sensitiveness of an old man as to his associates. Mather intimates [2] that it was jealousy of Hooker's abilities which broke off the negotiations. Mr. Paget, however, denies his responsibility for breaking them, and asserts that they were broken by the Classis and the Synod, and that the ground of this action was Mr. Hooker's position in willingness to accord fellowship to Brownists, and his refusing to censure such as "went to hear the 'Brownists' in their schismatical assembly." [3] This representation of Hooker's position Mather asserts is incorrect, averring [4] that instead of favouring the Brownists he had an "extream aversion" to them, and that he told Mr. Paget that to "separate from the faithful assemblies and churches in *England,* as no churches is an error in judgment, and a sin in practice, held and maintained by the *Brownists;* and therefore to communicate with them in their opinions or practice is sinful and utterly unlawful; and care should be taken to prevent offence, either by encouraging them in their way, or by drawing others to a further approbation of that way than is meet."

If this statement were fully to be relied on, it would seem to be conclusive. But it is easy for controversialists to mistake one another. There is no evidence that up to this time Mr. Hooker had come in contact with the Brownists, or, as they came soon to be called. Independents, at all; and his views about their position may not have become in all respects defined. Certainly he came to be a strenuous Independent, and his leanings that way may have become clear enough for the recognition of his Presbyterian associate. At all events, it is certain that the Synod was some way led to pronounce an adverse judgment upon the question of his joint pastorate with Mr. Paget, declaring, in confirmation of the conclusion already reached by the Classis, "that a person's standing in such opinions as were in writing showed unto the Classis, could not with any edification be admitted at the Ministry of the English Church at Amsterdam." [5] The fact that Mr. Paget had similar troubles respecting the proposed association with him subsequently of Mr. Davenport, Mr. Parker, Mr. Forbes, and Mr. Peter, together with the result of these controversies in a wordy war of pamphlets, in which he and Mr. Davenport assailed each other in a style more vigorous than courteous, — Mr. Davenport accusing Mr. Paget of "Tyrannical Government and Corrupt Doctrine," and Mr. Paget countering with the accusation that Mr. Davenport had issued a book with a "vile title" and contents "also as vile," [6] — may perhaps justify Fuller's characterization [7] of Mr. Paget as a "captious Puritan," but goes far to absolve him of the meaner motive of personal jealousy which Mather intimates. For indeed the issues between the parties were the radical ones which afterward so divided on English soil the forces of Presbyterianism and Independency. Nor ought it to be forgotten in defence — or excuse, as one chooses — of the position of the occupants of English Presbyterian pulpits in Holland, that they were still under the watch and regulation of the government at home. In May, 1628, King Charles had addressed "to the Synod of the English and Scottish clergy in the Netherlands" a series of commands, [8] corresponding to those we have seen imposed on the ministry in England, requiring the "foresaid clergymen [not to] interfere, either in making or composing, ...any new Liturgy or fixed form of prayer for their congregations." They "shall introduce no novelties in any rites or ceremonies," and "they shall not presume to meddle with any points of doctrine." The situation of any occupant of a State-recognized pulpit in Holland was thus, it will be seen, about as embarrassing as that of any minister at home; and it is not strange that Mr. Paget should have found himself perplexed by the proposed association with him of men of as advanced and in some respects of as disagreeing opinions as Hooker and Parker and Davenport and Hugh Peter entertained among themselves.

Leaving Amsterdam, Mr. Hooker went to Delft, and became connected in the ministry of the Scottish Presbyterian Church there with its pastor, Rev. John Forbes. Here conditions were more favourable for a comfortable association with the established incumbent. Mr. Forbes had already experienced something of the severity of prerogative, having been banished from Scotland about 1611, for presiding as moderator of the famous Aberdeen Assembly called contrary to the wish of the king; and he had his own nonconforming inclinations, as was proved a little after the time of Hooker's connection with him, by his removal from his charge at the request of the British Government, for not submitting to the discipline which Laud was bent on extending over English residents abroad as well as in their own land. [9] Mather speaks [10] with his usual effusiveness of classical illustration of the relations existing during these two years between Mr. Forbes and Mr. Hooker, comparing them to "*Basil* and *Nazianzen, ...one soul in two bodies,*" but of positive incident records only the first preaching of Mr. Hooker at Delft, from the text, "To you it is given not only to believe, but also to suffer," — a topic certainly fruitful of illustration to many in those troublous times.

After about two years Mr. Hooker removed to Rotterdam, being invited to some kind of ministerial association with Rev. Hugh Peter and Rev. William Ames, though his name does not, like theirs, appear on the pastoral list of the church. This organization had been gathered apparently about the year 1628, by Peter, afterward to be so well known in New England story and destined to so tragic a fate in the civil war at home. And with him in 1632 was joined, to survive only a few months, the celebrated ex-professor of the Franeker University, best known to scholars by his Latinized name *Amesius,* Ames had again and again experienced the severity of English high-churchly ill-will, which had prevailed several times with the authorities of Holland to prevent his establishment in some position of honour to which he had been called; and now, worn out with labour and exposure to the North Sea winds of the province of Franeker, he came to Rotterdam to die. Indefatigable however as a writer, Ames was engaged at the time of his death on a book entitled "A Fresh Svit against Human Ceremonies in Gods Worship."

This book is an answer to one written by Dr. John Burgess, which itself was a rejoinder to a previous volume by Ames, published in 1622. Ames was Dr. Burgess's son-in-law, though his wife, Dr. Burgess's daughter, was dead before this controversy began. One wonders how far family feeling may have mingled with conscientious principle in this voluminous and protracted debate. But our chief concernment in the matter lies in the fact that as Ames barely lived to see the main part of his manuscript through the press, and even that under great difficulties, Mr. Hooker completed the task, writing "An Advertisment to the Reader, Occasioned by the never enough lamented death of my deare freind, the Authour of this Fresh suite." In this "Advertisment" he says of his friend: —

"Vnderstand Christian Reader, that with the comming forth of this booke into the light, the learned and famous Authour Dr. Ames left the light, or darknes rather of this world. ... I may not keep back what I heard him speake as in the sight of God, that he was in his conscience more perswaded of the evill of these reliques of Popery and monuments of that superstition then ever, and yet he never had seen good in them, or come from them; and that moreover if D. B. [Dr. Burgess] or any other of them would yet be daubing with untempered mortar, and not give over to paint rotten sepulchres, he was by the grace of God resolved still to maintain the cause, and while he liued never let fall the suit commenced this way. ...Together with his life God hath put an end to all his travailes, wherein he shewed himself a pattern of holines, a burning and a shining light, and lamp of learning & Arts, a Champion for trueth, specially while for the space of 12 yeares at least, he was in the Doctors Chaire at Franequer, and having fought the good fight of faith, whereunto he was called, & professed a good profession before many witnesses, he hath now indeed layd hold on eternall life."

With this estimate of Ames on Mr. Hooker's part, it is pleasant to know that Dr. Ames was wont to say of Mr. Hooker, that "though he had been acquainted with many scholars of divers nations, yet he never met with Mr. Hooker's equal, either for preaching or for disputing." [11] It is plain, too, that Mr. Hooker agreed with the argument and conclusions of Ames's book. Besides the "Advertisment" he wrote also the long Preface to the volume; a brief extract from which will sufficiently indicate his own position on the question in debate. He says: —

"The state of this warr is this: wee (as it becommeth Christians) stand upon the sufficiency of Christs institutions, for all kynde of worship: and that *exclusively the word* (say we) & *nothing but the word, in matters of Religious worship.* The Praelats rise up on the other side, & will needs haue us allowe, & use certayne humane Ceremonyes of Religion in our Christian worship. We desire to be excused, as houlding them unlawfull. Christ we know: & all that cometh from him, we are ready to imbrace. But these human Cerem. in divine worship wee know not, nor can haue any thing to doe with them."

One further quotation from this Preface written by Mr. Hooker is significant as indicating the trials which the demand for conformity occasioned both to those who resisted and to some who, in his opinion rather weakly, yielded to the demand. The quotation is the more significant because he prints in the margin against the passage the words, "I speake but what I know." He says: —

"Its certayne, some have openly protested, that, if it were but half an hovvres hanging, they would rather suffer it, then subscribe. But for them & theirs, to ly in the ditch, & to be cast into a blynd corner, like broken vessels; yea they & their familyes to dye many hundred deaths, by extreame misery, before they could come unto their graves; This they were not able to undergoe. A condition, I acknowledge, which needs & deserves a great deale of pity & commiseration, since it is true, that some kinds of oppression make a man mad: But oh that the God of mercy would put it into the mynds & hearts of those whom it doth concerne, that they would never suffer such refuse reliques, longe, to hazard, not only the comforts, but even the consciences & happines of many distressed soules."

The book was issued in 1633, and probably in the early part of it, for the seventh month of the year was to find Mr. Hooker across the seas, in America.

This transit to America must have been a good while contemplated. Apparently the original plan had been to associate Hooker and Cotton in a New England enterprise; a project, however, which had been abandoned, for the reason as Mather asserts that it was thought that "a couple of such great men might be more servicable asunder than together." It may have been in connection with this proposed union of these two eminent lights in some joint church-fellowship in a New World plantation that Hooker wrote to Cotton from Rotterdam: —

"The state of these provinces to my weak eye, seems wonderfully ticklish and miserable. For the better part, *heart religion,* they content themselves with very forms, though much blemished; but the power of godliness, for ought I can see or hear, they know not; and if it were thoroughly pressed, I fear least it will be fiercely opposed." [12]

But the hope for any improvement in Puritan prospects either in Holland or England was small. The hand of prerogative reached across the German Sea, and laid its heavy weight upon the churches there holding nominal connection with the State, and was annoying and disquieting those avowedly independent of such connections. Laud's influence was all the while growing at home; and the significant coincidence may be noted that it was this year (1633) that saw his elevation from the bishopric of London to the archbishopric of Canterbury and the primacy of all England. How the Roman Church regarded the English primate may be inferred from the fact, which he records in his diary, that eleven days after his elevation to his new dignity he was offered a cardinalate in the papal hierarchy. No wonder the Puritans were discouraged as to any relief in Holland or at home. Their thoughts turned to the New World as their only refuge.

Apparently plans had so far matured that a company of people had gone from Essex County the year before to America, and had settled down, temporarily at first, at Mount Wollaston, near Boston, with the expectancy of Mr. Hooker's following them. Already in August, 1632, this group of settlers from the towns and vicinity of Braintree, Colchester, and Chelmsford — the scene of Mr. Hooker's English ministry — were known as "Mr. Hooker's Company." [13] Mr. Hooker was then in Holland, and did not arrive for more than a year afterward; but it was doubtless in pursuance of an understanding that he was to follow that they bore his name and anticipated his coming. Removed shortly by order of Court to Newtown, they awaited the fulfilment of the arrangements which were to bring them a fully equipped ministry. This fully equipped ministry, as there will be occasion shortly to notice, demanded the service not of one, but of two preaching Elders, respectively named the Pastor and the Teacher of the church.

Consequently, when the negotiations for joining Mr. Hooker and Mr. Cotton had been abandoned, the "judicious Christians" who had the interests of Mr. Hooker and Mr. Hooker's American company in charge turned to younger men. Rev. John Norton, afterward of Ipswich and of Boston, and Rev. Thomas Shepard, subsequently of Cambridge and Mr. Hooker's son-in-law, were thought of; but choice fell finally upon Rev. Samuel Stone, then a Lecturer at Towcester.

Mr. Stone was born at Hertford, and baptized at All Saints Church there July 30, 1602. He was probably educated, at least in part, at Hale's Grammar School in his native place, which was endowed in 1617, when Master Samuel was about fifteen years old. He entered Emmanuel College as pensioner April 19, 1620, and took his B. A. degree in 1624, and his M. A. in 1627. The middle of June of that year found him exercising the functions of curate at the parish of All Saints at Stisted in Essex, two miles from Braintree, where the records till September, 1630, appear to be in his handwriting. Probably it was during this Stisted residence that he came into some kind of pupillary connection with Rev. Richard Blackerby, a graduate of Trinity College, Cambridge, "who, not being capable of a Benefice, because he could not subscribe," [14] established a school at Ashen, in the same county; constantly "kept Lectures in some Neighbouring Town," and became a kind of peripatetic theological seminary for nearly twenty-three years together. "Divers young Students (after they came from the University) betook themselves to him to prepare them for the Ministry, ...and many eminent persons proceeded from this *Gamaliel.*"

Sometime in 1630, however, Mr. Stone went as Puritan Lecturer to the considerable town of Towcester in Northampton. He went by the commendation of Thomas Shepard, who had himself been invited to the place. Shepard's commendation of Mr. Stone to the position he could not himself occupy was not based on any new acquaintance. Eight years before, when they were at Emmanuel together, Stone, who was the elder by about four years, had been Shepard's adviser in a matter of great concern to him, commending him to the "spiritual and excellent preaching of Dr. Preston." And Shepard records [15] that Mr. Stone went to Towcester with the Lecture, "where the Lord was with him. And thus I saw the Lord's mercy following me to make me a poor instrument of sending the Gospel to the place of my nativity."

It was during this occupancy of the Towcester Lectureship that Mr. Stone was invited by "the judicious Christians that were coming to *New-England* with Mr. *Hooker*," to be "an *assistant* unto Mr. *Hooker*, with something of a *disciple* also." [16] Sometime in 1633, therefore, Mr. Hooker crossed over from Holland to England, and joined his prospective colleague in the New England ministry.

One late incident of Mr. Hooker's experience in England remains in the quaint and pedantic narrative of Mather, which shows Mr. Stone to have been, as he has always had the credit of being, a man of ready wits. The place is not stated, but it may very possibly have been at Mr. Stone's family home at Hertford. The story may be told in the language of the "Magnalia": [17] —

"Returning into *England* order to a further voyage, he [Mr. Hooker] was quickly scented by the pursevants; who at length got so far up with him, as to knock at the door of that very chamber, where he was now discoursing with Mr. *Stone;* who was now become his designed companion and assistant for the *New-English* enterprize. Mr. Stone was at that instant smoking of *tobacco;* for which Mr. Hooker had been reproving him, as being then used by few persons of sobriety; being also of a sudden and pleasant wit, he stept unto the door, with his pipe in his mouth, and such an air of speech and look, as gave him some credit with the officer. The officer demanded, *Whether Mr.* Hooker *were not there?* Mr. *Stone* replied with a braving sort of confidence, *What* Hooker? *Do you mean* Hooker *that lived once at* Chelmsford! The officer answered, *Yes, he!* Mr. *Stone* immediately, with a diversion like that which once helped *Athanasius,* made this true answer. *If it be he you look for, I saw him about an hour ago, at such an house in town; you had best hasten thither after him.* The officer took this for a sufficient account, and went his way; but Mr. *Hooker,* upon this intimation, concealed himself more carefully and securely, till he went on board, at the *Downs,* in the year 1633, the ship which brought him, and Mr. *Cotton,* and Mr. *Stone* to *New-England:* where none but Mr. Stone was owned for a preacher, at their first coming aboard; the other two delaying to take their turns in the publick worship of the ship, till they were got so far into the main ocean, that they might with safety, discover who they were."

The voyage was of eight weeks' duration. It was doubtless diversified, as we know from Roger Clap's Diary [18] the Dorchester company's voyage was, by the "preaching or expounding of the word of God every day" by some one of the ministers. And there was certainly considerable preaching capacity on board the "Griffin," and a good deal of hearing capacity also; for beside Hooker and Stone, Rev. John Cotton was of the company, and Mr. Pierce, Mr. Haynes, afterward Governor of Massachusetts and of Connecticut, "a gentleman of great estate, Mr. Hoffe [Atherton Hough] and many other men of good estates," two hundred passengers in all, were fellow voyagers. [19] The incident of the birth of a child to Mr. Cotton on the voyage is recorded, and is chiefly memorable for the occasion it gave for the indication of the quite pronounced type of Congregationalism which prevailed among the "Griffin's" company, manifested in withholding the rite of baptism from the poor infant till land was reached and a new church-membership could be established.

The vessel reached Boston September 4; and "Mr. Hooker and Mr. Stone went presently to Newtown, where they were to be entertained, and Mr. Cotton stayed at Boston." [20] On the following Saturday, Mn and Mrs. Cotton were "propounded to be admitted" members of the Boston church. On the Sunday after, they were admitted; and then the child was presented by his father and baptized "Seaborn" by Rev. Mr. Wilson, pastor of the church; Mr. Cotton explaining that the reason why the child had not been baptized on the voyage was "not for want of fresh water, for he held, sea-water would have served," but "1., because they had no settled congregation there; 2, because a minister hath no power to give the seals but in his own congregation." [21] This is certainly very vigorous Congregationalism. Cotton and Hooker and Stone, who were doubtless at one in this view, had manifestly thrown overboard a large cargo of ecclesiastical traditions in which they had been educated.

This practical breach with the system of things left behind doubtless received additional illustration when, on the nth of October following, Mr. Hooker and Mr. Stone were ordained respectively Pastor and Teacher of the church at Newtown. Not that the Newtown company, any more than the Salem company, led by Francis Higginson four years before, was an avowedly Separatist company. It was Puritan. Its members had probably every one been members of the established Church of England. It is not likely that any of them while in their own country had stood in a position of declared Separation from it. But three thousand miles of watery distance from a hierarchy many of whose usages they had cast off, and plantation in a virgin wilderness, were great realities which could not be forgotten when the fashioning of new ecclesiastical institutions came to be forced upon them. Hence when the new settlers of Massachusetts Bay came to the formation of their churches, they did, as a matter of fact, adopt the Brownist theory, already illustrated ten years or more at Plymouth, of the competency of every congregation of believers to constitute its own church-estate, and to choose and ordain its own officers. Indeed, in the very first instance of the constitution of such a church within the province of Massachusetts — that at Salem in 1629 — the influence and co-operation of the avowedly Separatist and Independent church of Plymouth is distinctly recognized. [22]

The church body to which Mr. Hooker and Mr. Stone came, had probably been organized before the arrival of the expected minister. It had been fourteen months on the ground; had erected a "house for public worship" with the very unusual accompaniment of "a bell upon it" some time in 1632; [23] had probably already adopted a covenant, chosen William Goodwin its Ruling Elder, and may have chosen Andrew Warner and some one else its Deacons. When it came to setting Pastor and Teacher in their offices the event took place doubtless in a way substantially identical with the like event occurring the day previous in the Boston church in the induction to office of John Cotton. That event Mr. Winthrop minutely describes. [24] Of this one, because he had so fully delineated the first, he simply says, under date of Oct. 11, 1633: "A fast at Newtown, where Mr. Hooker was chosen pastor, and Mr. Stone teacher, in such a manner as before at Boston." That procedure becomes thus a guide in the present transaction at Newtown. In the light of it no essential mistake can be made if it is said to have taken place as follows. A Ruling Elder and two Deacons having been chosen — either at that time or, as the weight of evidence seems to show, previously — the "congregation" signified, in response to the proposal by the Ruling Elder, their choice of Mr. Hooker as Pastor, and of Mr. Stone as Teacher, by the "erection of hands." Then the Ruling Elder asked the two elected officers if they did "accept of that call," whereto, if they answered as Cotton did at Boston, they in effect replied that knowing themselves to be "unworthy and unsufficient for that place; yet, having observed all the passages of God's providence in calling [them] to it, [they] could not but accept it." Whereupon, in default of a Preaching Elder such as was had in Mr. Cotton's case to join with the Ruling Elder in the service, the Ruling Elder with "3 or 4 of ye gravest members of ye church" — as in Higginson's and Skelton's ordination at Salem — laid their hands on Mr. Hooker's head, and the Ruling Elder prayed, and then, "taking off their hands, laid them on again, and, speaking to him by his name, they did thenceforth design him to the said office [of pastor] in the name of the Holy Ghost." The Pastor being thus ordained and now taking the lead, he and the Ruling Elder and some "grave member" laid their hands on the head of Mr. Stone, and with similar service of prayer, declaration of office, and sign of enduement of the Holy Ghost, ordained him to the office of Teacher. Then if Mr. Wilson, Mr. Cotton, or other "neighboring ministers" were present, as was probably the case, they gave the new Pastor and Teacher the "right hands of fellowship."

And so the church at Newtown became fully equipped and officered for its work; being, if we must suppose it not organized till this date of Oct. 11, 1633, the tenth or eleventh church gathered on this New England soil; but if organized before, as was more likely the fact, being, as Johnson says in his "Wonder-Working Providence," the "eighth." [25]

Pastor and Teacher, — the distinction between these two officers in the primitive New England church was supposed to be based on Scripture, as for example on Ephesians iv. 11, and to be practically important. This distinction is perhaps as well stated as anywhere in an "Answer" of certain "Reverend Brethren" in New England, sent in 1639, to inquiries addressed to them in 1637 by "many Puritan ministers" in Old England; the twenty-second of which inquiries was this, "What Essentiall difference put you between the Office of Pastor and Teacher, and doe you observe the same difference inviolably?" To which inquiry this reply was given, [26] "And for the Teacher and Pastor, the difference between them lyes in this, that the one is principally to attend upon points of Knowledge and Doctrine, though not without Application; the other to points of Practice, though not without Doctrine." Both were preachers, but the Pastor's function as a preacher was thought to have special reference to the experimental part of life and behaviour; the Teacher's rather to dogma and faith. Both had oversight of the flock; but the Pastor was supposed to be the shepherd and feeder, the Teacher the guide and warder. Both were to be vigilant against error; but the Pastor chiefly in matters of practice, the Teacher in matters of belief. Both gave their whole time to the work of the ministry, and were supported by the common funds of the congregation.

Yet it is obvious that the distinction between these two offices was an obscure one, and that each was likely to be continually taking on the functions of the other. The Pastor could not preach much without dealing with matters of doctrine, and the Teacher could not instruct long without dealing with matters of practice. So that it is not surprising that this supposed important distinction between the pastoral and teaching function — though lasting longer in general New England history than the ruling eldership — became before a very great while obsolete.

But in that first new day of ecclesiastical experiment and devotion, Pastor and Teacher were deemed alike indispensable. And so the "grave godly and judicious *Hooker*, ...and the Retoricall, Mr. *Stone*" [27] entered upon the work of the two offices side by side.

[1] Steven's Scottish Church in Rotterdam, p. 273.
[2] Magualia, i. 307, 308.
[3] Hanbury, i. 532, 541.
[4] Magnalia, i. 308.
[5] Hanbury, i. 532.
[6] Ibid. 527.
[7] Church History, book xi. p. 51.
[8] Steven, pp. 262, 263.
[9] Steven, p. 294.

[10] Magnalia, i. 308.
[11] Magnalia, i. 308.
[12] Magnalia, i. 308.
[13] Winthrop's Journal, i. 104, 105.
[14] Clark's Lives, p. 58.
[15] Young's Massachusetts, p. 518.
[16] Magnalia, i. 393.
[17] Ibid 309.
[18] Young's Massachusetts, p, 348.
[19] Winthrop, i. 129, 130.
[20] Ibid. 130.
[21] Ibid. 131.
[22] Bradford's History, pp. 264, 265; Magnalia, i. 66.
[23] Prince's Annals, ii. 75; Hubbard, p. 189; Paige's Cambridge, p. 17.
[24] Journal, i. 135, 136.
[25] Wonder-Working Providence, p. 60.
[26] Church Government and Church Covenant Discussed (written by Richard Mather), etc., pp. 74-76.
[27] Wonder-Working Providence, p. 58.

Chapter Five – In Massachusetts and Removal to Connecticut

For after Mr. Hooker's coming over, it was observed that many of the freemen grew to be very jealous of their liberties.

Hubbard (ed. 1848), p. 165.

The communitary life into which Pastor Hooker and Teacher Stone found themselves introduced on their arrival in the Bay had already passed the severest of the experiences incident to the planting of a new colony. Salem, Dorchester, Boston, Watertown, Roxbury, Lynn, Charlestown, and probably Newtown had not only regularly established town organizations, but church institutions and more or less well-developed social privileges; and there were several other plantations in the near vicinity which were moving rapidly toward a like stage of development.

All these various settlements in the Bay had grown up since 1628, when, after several ineffectual attempts to plant permanent institutions, a company of settlers under the lead of John Endicott had fixed upon Salem, and made there the hoped-for dwelling-place of "peace."

These towns were all gathered under the provisions of a charter to the "Governor and Company of the Massachusetts Bay," granted in 1629, which document had been brought over by Mr. John Winthrop and a notable company of associates in June, 1630. The granting of the charter was as a trumpet-call to sympathizers with the Puritan movement in England; and company after company of stalwart men and heroic women, despairing of the reformation of the State and Church in their own land, turned their faces in hope to the New World, and found home and sanctuary in more or less voluntary exile in America.

Probably at the time of Hooker's arrival at Newtown at least three thousand Englishmen were scattered among the towns and plantations of the

Bay. They were settling down to the various labours of planting, building, making roads and bridges, catching and curing fish, trading with the Indians for furs, taking care of their flocks of sheep and goats, breeding cattle, and building up the fabric of an orderly society. It was, on the whole, a remarkable assemblage of men and women.

The ministers, now numbering thirteen or fourteen in the colony, were nearly all University men, had been clergy of the English Church, and were, several of them, eminent at home for all clerical gifts and attainments. The magistrates were men of good social position in their own land, and some of them of wealth and honourable family. The rank and file of the citizenship were of solid, middle-class English life, — men and women thrifty, sober, conscientious, intelligently religious, and Puritan by conviction and experience. It was a strong, hardy, somewhat stern and austere society, as became people who had had trials, were in the midst of hardships, and had the prospect of difficulties yet before them.

The particular town to which Hooker came had, in the autumn of 1633, about a hundred families. It had been intended that the place should be the seat of government; and in 1630 some houses had been built, and a "pallysadoe" made "aboute the newe towne," and a "fosse" — some of whose remains were visible at the beginning of the present century — dug about the designated precincts of the fortifications. The superior advantages of Boston, however, as the main town of the colony, caused the abandonment of the plan for fortifying Newtown; but William Wood, writing in the year Hooker arrived, describes the place as "one of the neatest and best compacted towns in New-England, having many fair structures, with many handsome contrived streets. The inhabitants, most of them, are very rich, and well stored with cattle of all sorts, having many hundred acres of ground paled in with one general fence, which is about a mile and a half long, which secures all their weaker cattle from the wild beasts." [1] These fair structures and handsome-contrived streets must be understood in the light of certain orders on the records of the little settlement, — that "all the houses [within] the bounds of the town shall be covered [with] slate or board, and not with thatch," and that all houses shall "range even, and stand just six [feet on each man's] own ground from the street." [2]

The coming of so marked a reinforcement of the ministry of the Bay as was implied in the arrival of Cotton, Hooker, and Stone was a source of profound rejoicing to the whole colony. Punning does not seem to have been a forbidden amusement \ for the people were pleased to say that their "three great necessities were now supplied, for they had Cotton for their clothing, Hooker for their fishing, and Stone for their building."

The ministers themselves instituted a meeting "at one of their houses by course, where some question of moment was debated." This meeting — the probable progenitor of the Boston Association of Congregational Ministers — was, however, looked, upon askance by Mr. Skelton, the pastor at Salem, and by Roger Williams, who was with him, "exercising by way of prophecy;" they "fearing it might grow in time to a presbytery or superintendency, to the prejudice of the churches' liberties." [3] Special religious awakening at Boston followed the coming of Mr. Cotton to the church in that place; and it was probably at this time that the Thursday lectures were established in each of the four nearly adjacent towns, — Boston, Dorchester, Roxbury, and Newtown. But by October of the following year (1634), "it being found, that the four lectures did spend too much time, and proved overburdensome to the ministers and people, the ministers, with the advice of the magistrates, ...did agree to reduce them to two days, viz., Mr. Cotton at Boston one Thursday, or the 5th day of the week, and Mr. Hooker at Newtown the next 5th day, and 'Mr. Warham at Dorchester one 4th day of the week, and Mr. Welde at Roxbury the next 4th day." [4] Apparently, however, this arrangement did not long suit the people, who then, as generally, liked to get all they could out of their ministers; and in December following the old practice of the afternoon lectures in each town was resumed. [5] The range of these Thursday lectures, if we may judge from the reports preserved of those of Mr. Cotton, swept the whole field of manners and morals as well as doctrine. One of these, in 1633 at Boston, was about the non-necessity of veils for women. Mr. Endicott, the fervid magistrate of Salem, who had been persuaded otherwise by Roger Williams, being present, argued against Mr. Cotton, adducing the commandment of "the apostle;" and the discussion grew so warm that the governor, Winthrop, felt called on to interpose, "and so it break off." [6]

At another lecture Mr. Cotton, being moved by complaints of the sharp dealing of Robert Keaine, a merchant of Boston, laid open the error of some "false principles" in matters of trade; one of which false principles was "that a man might sell as dear as he can, and buy as cheap as he can;" another, "that he may sell as he bought, though he paid too dear, etc., and though the commodity be fallen." Against which he laid down the proposition, among others, that "a man may not ask any more for his commodity than his selling price, as Ephron to Abraham, the land is worth thus much." [7] At still another lecture Mr. Cotton came down in reproval of a proposition pending in the General Court for leaving out of office "two of their ancientest magistrates, because they were grown poor," censuring "such miscarriage," and telling the "country, that such as were decayed in their estates by attending the service of the country ought to be maintained by the country." [8] But the staple of Mr. Cotton's lectures was Scripture exposition and application. He had practised the same thing at his lectures in England, and "at both Bostons went through near the whole Bible." [9] Mr. Cotton's Thursday lectures were probably in topic and method essentially the same with those of other ministers of the colony. We know more of them than we do of Mr. Hooker's or the other ministers' mainly because he had in his church an intelligent hearer who kept a journal. Mr. Hooker had no Governor Winthrop jotting down in his diary the current events in which his pastor took a share. Nevertheless he seems to have been concerned and influential in most matters that were going on. In 1633 and again in 1636 he was associated with Cotton and Wilson in reconciling certain oppositions of the somewhat touchy Mr. Dudley of Newtown and Governor Winthrop of Boston, — once on some personal difference, [10] and again about the degree of leniency allowable in the administration of public affairs, [11] Dudley being in favour of sterner measures than Winthrop practised or desired. On the second of these occasions, Mr. Haynes of Newtown, then governor, sided against the lenient conduct of Winthrop, — a fact to be made note of in connection with questions shortly to arise concerning the causes of the separation of the Newtown Company from the colony. In November, 1634, the Assistants called on Mr. Hooker, with Mr. Cotton and Mr. Welde of Roxbury, to take to task his old acquaintance, the usher of the Little Baddow School, John Eliot, — then the young Teacher of the Roxbury church and afterward the Indian Apostle, — for criticising the magistrates as to their manner of making peace with the Pequots. [12]

More memorable was another transaction in which the General Court invoked Mr. Hooker's aid. The restless and afterward celebrated Roger Williams had been installed in Mr. Skelton's place at Salem against the remonstrance of the magistrates of the colony, [13] who already — in 1631 — had had experience of his disquieting influence in that place. Since that time he had been in Plymouth ventilating such unsettled judgments as made the Plymouth church in commending him back to the Salem fellowship accompany their commendation "with some caution to them concerning him, and what care they ought to have of him." [14] Arrived at Salem again, he recommenced the controversies which ultimately resulted in his sentence of banishment. It was the circumstances of the time which gave to Mr. Williams's performances their special dangerousness. No doctrinal question of religion was involved, least of all that view of baptism which he afterward — and temporarily [15] — held, and which has so often erroneously been represented as a cause of exclusion from the colony. He denied the validity of the colonial charter; [16] he counselled the cutting out of the cross from the king's flag; [17] he declared the administration of an oath of office to an unregenerate person to be a participation in taking "the name of God in vain;" [18] he pronounced worship in churches which had not renounced connection with the Established Church of England a sin. [19] When the General Court suspended action on a petition of Salem to receive a grant of public land, he moved his church to write to other churches to discipline their members who as town-representatives united in this delay; [20] when these churches hesitated to act on this advice of the Salem church, he counselled his church to withdraw fellowship from them; [21] when his church did not act on his counsel in this matter, he withdrew fellowship from it, and set up a private conventicle in his own house; [22] and when his wife continued to attend the Salem church, he renounced fellowship with her, and refused to say family prayers or grace at the table in her presence. [23] In an established time of quietude these performances of Mr. Williams might have been comparatively harmless, and been winked at as tokens only of the unsettled judgment which the clear mind of Governor Bradford had already noted. But it was not a time of quiet. The liberties of the colony were in imminent peril. Proceedings had already commenced for vacating the charter in the English courts. Reports tending to inflame the ecclesiastical authorities in England were continually sent back by disaffected persons, in America. In this condition of affairs, to deny the charter's validity, to charge the king with telling a "lie" in granting it, [24] to recommend the mutilation of the king's colours, to proclaim the unchristian character of the churches in not denouncing the English Church as anti-Christian, and to turmoil the churches and magistrates among themselves, were offences against civil peace which no administration could overlook. The question was not theological, it was a question of political order and of public safety; [25] and it was forced upon a reluctant government by a man who was not even a freeman of the colony, but one who personally declined, and employed his pulpit to induce others to decline, even a resident's oath of loyalty to the government under which he lived.

Being summoned before the Court in October, 1635, Mr. Williams "maintained all his opinions." Asked if he would take the subject into further thought, for which purpose a month's consideration was proposed to him, he refused, choosing to "dispute presently."

Accepting his proposal, Mr. Hooker was requested to argue the points in debate, in hope of securing acquiescence to avoid extremer measures. Most of the discussion has perished. One point of it, however, in which Mr. Hooker apparently attempted to apply to Mr. Williams's doctrine of the sinfulness of tendering an oath to an unregenerate person the method known as the *reductio ad absurdum,* remains in Mr. Cotton's account of it. [26] Mr. Williams had complained —

"that he was wronged by a slanderous report up and downe the Countrey, as if he did hold it to be unlawfull for a Father to call upon his childe to eat his meate. Our reverend Brother, Mr. Hooker, (the Pastor of the Church where the Court was then kept) being mooved to speake a word to it, Why, saithe he, you will say as much againe (if you stand to your own Principles) or be forced to say nothing. When Mr. Williams was confident he should never say it, Mr. Hooker replyed, If it be unlawfull to Call an unregenerate person to take an Oath, or to Pray, as being actions of God's worship, then it is unlawfull for your unregenerate childe to pray for a blessing upon his own meate. If it be unlawfull for him to pray for a blesing upon his meate, it is unlawfull for him to eate it (for it is sanctified by prayer, and without prayer unsanctified, *I Tim. iv*: 4, 5.) If it be unlawfull for him to eate it, it is unlawfull for you to call upon him to eate it, for it is unlawfull for you to call upon him to sinne. — Here Mr. Williams thought better to hold his peace, then to give an Answer."

The "dispute" had the general issue of similar controversies. Mr. Hooker's endeavours were well meant, and judging from this sample were logically ingenious in putting Mr. Williams into an uncomfortable dilemma, but he "could not reduce him from any of his errors."

The inevitable consequence followed. Mr. Williams's teachings and behaviour were playing directly into the hands of Laud and prerogative abroad, and schism and disorder at home; and the order of Court was that he leave the colony, whose lawful right to be or to legislate he denounced, within the six weeks next ensuing.

Reference has been made to the mutilation of the national ensign. Though encouraged by Williams, the act was that of Endicott. The matter made a great stir. The towns were called on to choose a commission of one from each town on the subject, to which commission the magistrates added four. The commission declared Mr Endicott's "offence to be great;" his action in denouncing the cross as "a sin" impeaching the magistrates as "if they would suffer idolatry," and "giving occasion to the state of England to think ill of us." Mr. Endicott was therefore admonished, and "disabled for one year from bearing any public office; "the magistrates declining "any heavier sentence, because they were persuaded he did it out of tenderness of conscience, and not of any evil intent." [27]

A sensible, quiet-tempered paper on this controversy was written by Mr. Hooker, which is preserved In the Massachusetts Historical Society's archives. It has never been published in full, but its general bearing may be inferred from the single paragraph:

"Not that I am a friend to the crosse as an idoll, or to any idollatry in it; or that any carnall fear takes me asyde and makes me unwilling to give way to the evidence of the truth, because of the sad consequences that may be suspected to flowe from it. I blesse the Lord, my conscience accuseth me of no such thing; but that as yet I am not able to see the sinfulness of this banner in a civil use."

The ministers of the colony were not eligible to secular office, but their advice was sought on weighty occasions, and Mr. Hooker's seems to have been prized as highly as that of any one. His church prospered as well as any church in the colony; its leading lay member, Mr. John Haynes, was chosen governor in May, 1635, on which occasion he signalized his liberality and ability alike by declining the usual salary of the office. [28] The town was as flourishing as any in the Bay, its tax being as large as Boston's. [29]

But all along, from very near the arrival of the "Griffin's" company, a certain uneasiness manifested itself in respect to the Newtown people's situation, all the causes of which are difficult to trace, but which culminated at last in the removal of Mr. Hooker and nearly the entire population of the town to Hartford. Only six months after the induction of Hooker and Stone into their offices the inhabitants of "Newtown complained [May, 1634] of straitness for want of land, especially meadow, and desired leave of the court to look out either for enlargement or removal, which was granted; whereupon they sent men to see Agawam and Merimack, and gave out that they would remove." [30] But apparently the Agawam and Merrimac reconnoissance was not satisfactory, for in July following they sent a pioneer party of six to Connecticut, "intending to remove their town thither." [31]

In September the matter came up again in the General Court. Winthrop gives this account of it: [32]

"September 4, the general court began at Newtown, and continued a week, and then was adjourned fourteen days. Many things were there agitated and concluded. ...But the main business, which spent the most time, and caused the adjourning of the court, was about the removal of Newtown. They had leave, the last general court, to look out some place for enlargement or removal, with promise of having it confirmed to them, if it were not prejudicial to any other plantation; and now they moved that they might have leave to remove to Connecticut. The matter was debated divers days, and many reasons alleged pro and con. The principal reasons for their removal were, 1. Their want of accommodation for their cattle, so as they were not able to maintain their ministers, nor could receive any more of their friends to help them; and here it was alleged by Mr. Hooker, as a fundamental error, that towns were set so near to each other. 2. The fruitfulness and commodiousness of Connecticut, and the danger of having it possessed by others, Dutch or English. 3. The strong bent of their spirits to remove thither.

"Against these it was said, 1. That, in point of conscience, they ought not to depart from us, being knit to us in one body, and bound by oath to seek the welfare of this commonwealth. 2. That, in point of state and civil policy, we ought not to give them leave to depart, i. Being we were now weak and in danger to be assailed. 2. The departure of Mr. Hooker would not only draw many from us, but also divert other friends that would come to us. 3. We should expose them to evident peril, both from the Dutch (who made claim to the same river, and had already built a fort there) and from the Indians, and also from our own state at home, who would not endure they should sit down without a patent in any place which our king lays claim unto. 3. They might be accommodated at home by some enlargement which other towns offered. 4. They might remove to Merrimack, or any other place within our patent. 5. The removing of a candlestick is a great judgement, which is to be avoided. Upon these and other arguments the court being divided, it was put to vote; and, of the deputies, fifteen were for their departure, and ten against it. The governour [Dudley] and two assistants were for it, and the deputy and all the rest of the assistants were against it, (except the secretary, who gave no vote;) whereupon no record was entered, because there were not six assistants in the vote, as the patent requires. Upon this grew a great difference between the governour and assistants, and the deputies. They would not yield the assistants a negative voice, and the others (considering how dangerous it might be to the commonwealth, if they should not keep that strength to balance the greater number of the deputies) thought it safe to stand upon it. So, when they could proceed no farther, the whole court agreed to keep a day of humiliation to seek the Lord, which accordingly was done, in all the congregations, the 18th day of this month; and the 24th the court met again. Before they began Mr. Cotton preached, (being desired by all the court, upon Mr. Hooker's instant excuse of his unfitness for that occasion). [33] He took his text out of Hag. II. 4, etc., out of which he laid down the nature or strength (as he termed it) of the magistracy, ministry, and people, viz., — the strength of the magistracy to be their authority; of the people, their liberty; and of the ministry, their purity; and showed how all of these had a negative voice, etc., and that yet the ultimate resolution, etc., ought to be in the whole body of the people, etc., with answer to all objections, and a declaration of the people's duty and right to maintain their true liberties against any unjust violence, etc., which gave great satisfaction to the company. And it pleased the Lord so to assist him, and to bless his own ordinance, that the affairs of the court went on cheerfully; and although all were not satisfied about the negative voice to be left to the magistrates, yet no man moved aught about it, and the congregation of Newtown came and accepted of such enlargement as had formerly been offered them by Boston and Watertown; and so the fear of their removal to Connecticut was removed."

It was on the occasion of this court — and it affords an indication of the excitement of the parties in interest — that the "very reverend and godly" Mr. William Goodwin, "elder of the congregation of Newtown," was reproved for his "unreverend speech to one of the assistants" in open court.

Things now seemed amicably adjusted. The enlargements granted to Newtown embraced the territory now known as the towns of Brookline, Brighton, Newton, and Arlington. Making every allowance for the necessities of a hundred families, even of an agricultural and cattle-raising class, this territory certainly seems sufficient. The population now dwelling on the same soil is upward of eighty thousand. But the settlers were not easy. "The strong bent of their spirits to remove" continued. Some cause deeper than any lack of land in five townships to pasture the cattle of a few settlers in the third year of their arrival must have impelled to this restlessness. What was it?

The historian Hubbard, writing within fifty years of these events, and while people still lived who were personally actors in them, says that other motives than deficiency of land did "more secretly and powerfully drive on the business." "Some men," he continues, "do not well like, at least, cannot well bear, to be opposed in their judgments and notions, and thence were they not unwilling to remove from under the power, as well as out of the bounds, of the Massachusetts." [34] "Two such eminent stars, such as were Mr. Cotton and Mr. Hooker, both of the first magnitude, though of differing influence, could not well continue in one and the same orb." [35] Dr. Benjamin Trumbull, in speaking of the death of Mr. Haynes, intimates that considerations arising from the relative influence of Haynes and Winthrop were not without weight. Mr. Haynes, he says, "was not considered, in any respect, inferior to Governor Winthrop. His growing popularity, and the fame of Mr. Hooker, who, as to strength of genius, and his lively and powerful manner of preaching, rivalled Mr. Cotton, were supposed to have no small influence upon the general court, in their granting liberty to Mr. Hooker and his company to remove to Connecticut." [36]

Some excellent writers have seemed quite unwilling to recognize in the actors in these events any such feelings, uttered or unexpressed, as are suggested in these statements of Hubbard and Trumbull. But nothing could be more natural, and few things are more probable.

Nevertheless the existence of such feelings, supposing them to exist, had doubtless their origin and occasion in matters lying deeper than merely personal ones. It seems clear that on certain important administrative questions the people who surrounded Mr. Hooker entertained different convictions from those prevalent in the Bay counsels generally. The Bay settlement was a distinctly theocratic society, in which civil franchise was contingent on church-membership. When Hooker arrived in Newtown, though the population of the colony was numbered by the thousands, the freemen of it were only about three hundred and fifty. [37] The principle of a state-church which Puritans had suffered from so much at home was, in fact, reestablished by them in the new land. [38] This contingency of civil privileges on church-connection was never adopted in the Connecticut Colony; and whether openly objected to or not by the men who founded Connecticut while yet they remained in Massachusetts, there can be no doubt that it was inwardly disapproved. Strong evidence that this question had its influence, as well as of Mr. Hooker's attitude upon it, remains in a letter written to Rev. John Wilson from England in the early spring after the removal to Connecticut had taken place, in which the writer speaks of having heard "That ther is great diuision of judgment in matters of religion amongst good ministers & people which moued Mr. Hoker to remoue;" and "That you are so strict in admission of members to your church, that more then halfe are out of your church in all your congregations, & that Mt. Hoker befor he went away preached against ye (as one reports who hard him)." [39]

With a difference of judgment in a matter so fundamental, other differences easily allied themselves. A distinct diversity of conception of the "authority of the magistrates" was clearly developed at the Court of September, 1634, between the Newtown party and the party opposed to removal. [40] Open and free disagreement between Mr. Haynes and Governor Winthrop as to administrative policy found expression in January, 1636, and had been taken cognizance of by all the ministers and magistrates, who had put themselves on one side or other of the point in debate. Add to this the danger impending that the charter of the colony might be withdrawn, and there seem to be ample grounds for believing that Mr. Haynes and Mr. Goodwin and the leading laymen of Newtown felt that they would be more comfortable under an administration of their own, in some other quarter of the boundless new land.

Nor is it improbable that Mr. Hooker shared the feeling on personal as well as political grounds. Before he left England overtures had been made by his friends, acting at Mr. Hooker's motion, [41] to secure Mr. Cotton as colleague with him in the proposed enterprise to America. The overture was declined. But on the arrival together in the new country of the two old acquaintances — and doubtless always friends — the colony seems to have been thrown into a kind of ferment as to the proper disposal of Mr. Cotton. Thirteen days after he landed the Governor and Council and all the ministers were called together "to consider about Mr. Cotton his sitting down." [42] Boston was fixed on as the "fittest place;" and it was first agreed that the payment for his weekly lectures should be out of the public treasury. This resolve was presently revoked as being invidious in its discrimination, but it indicates the feeling of the hour.

Established thus with the acclaim of the magistracy and of the people in the central point of ecclesiastical influence in the colony, the great abilities and tireless industry of Mr. Cotton pervaded everything. "Whatever he delivered in the pulpit was soon put into an Order of Court, if of a civil, or set up as a practice in the church, if of an ecclesiastical concernment." [43] And Mr. Cotton's political deliverances were generally on the side of authority and permanency in the magistracy; a side to which the general tendencies of the Newtown pastor's mind did not equally lead him. On the critical occasion of the hearing before the Court in September, 1634, of the great question of the removal — when Mr. Hooker somewhat unaccountably excused himself from preaching on the issues raised by the Newtown proposal — Mr. Cotton's effort apparently settled the business on the side of the Assistants, and adversely to the Newtown party.

So that on the whole it is neither strange nor at all discreditable, that the Newtown company should have thought themselves likely to be happier and more useful in some other settlement than that to which the Court had ordered them in 1632. Conscious of the possession of laymen as able as any in the colony, and of a minister of as great qualities as any other, their "strong bent" to remove continued, and finally prevailed.

Some of them apparently went to Connecticut before September, 1635; for on the 3d of that month William Westwood was "sworn Constable of the plantations at Connecticut till some other be chosen," [44] — a procedure hardly reconcilable with the theory maintained in the arguments before the Court in September previous that the settlers there would be without the Massachusetts patent. [45] Others soon followed. These settlers of 1635 suffered immense hardships along the banks of the great river, which froze over that season by the 15th of November. Famine and cold seemed to conspire against the enterprise. Cattle died; the people had to resort to acorns for food. Except for the succour afforded by Indians, many must have perished. [46]

But these hardships were not to deter the main body of the Newtown pilgrims; when spring came again, the rest of the company were ready for flight.

Fortunately the arrival, the autumn previous, of a large number of immigrants into the Bay, and the gathering of a considerable part of them into church-relationship under the pastoral care of Rev. Thomas Shepard on the 1st of February, 1636, enabled the Newtown people to sell their houses to the newcomers. On the 3d of March, 1636, John Steele and William Westwood were appointed among the eight commissioners empowered by Massachusetts to "govern the people at Connecticutt." These commissioners were either then in Connecticut or speedily after, as five of them, including Steele and Westwood, held a "Corte...att Newton [Hartford] 26 Apr. 1636." [47]

The 31st of May saw the emigrants upon their journey. It is the season of the year in our New England climate when the billowy expanses of our forests are bursting into leaf, and each day marks a visible deepening of colour and density in the landscape verdure. The streams run full with the newly melted snows of winter. The ground is spotted with the anemone and wild violet. In the marshy places glow the adder-tongue and the cowslip. The season is alive with promise; but the nights, though short, are damp and chill.

The Newtown pilgrims struck out into the almost pathless woods. Only a few miles from their place of brief habitation, and they were in a wilderness marked only by signs of Indian trails. Evening by evening they made camp and slept, guarded and sentinelled, by forest fires. One of their number, Mrs. Hooker, the pastor's wife, was carried on a litter because of her infirmity. It was a picturesque but an arduous pilgrimage. Men and women of refinement and delicate breeding turned explorers of primeval forests in search of a wilderness home. The lowing of a hundred and sixty cattle sounding through the forest aisles, not to mention the bleating of goats and the squealing of swine, summoned them to each morning's advance. The day began and ended with the voice of prayer and perhaps of song. At some point on their fortnight's journey a Sabbath must have intervened, when of course the camp remained still for worship in the wilderness. Their toilsome and devious way led them probably by the route which came to be known as the "old Connecticut path," through what were afterward the towns of Framing ham and Dudley and Woodstock; the same route by which the roving Oldham went in 1633, when he lodged in "Indian towns all the way." Reaching at some uncertain point the wide, full Connecticut, flowing then with larger tide than now, and swollen with its northern snows, the travellers crossed on rafts and rudely constructed boats; and on the spot where Hartford now lifts its stately edifices of worship and of trade, and cheered by the sight of some pioneer attempts at habitation and settlement made the season previous, "Mr. Hooker's company" rested, and the ark of the church stood still.

[1] "New England's Prospect," in Young's Massachusetts, p. 402.

[2] Paige's Cambridge, pp. 18, 19.

[3] Winthrop, i. 139.

[4] Winthrop, 1. 172.
[5] Ibid. 180.
[6] Ibid. 149.
[7] Winthrop, i. 378-382.
[8] Ibid. ii. 67.
[9] Cotton's Narrative, 4 Mass. Hist. Coll., iv. 284.
[10] Winthrop, i. 139, 140.
[11] Ibid. 212.
[12] Winthrop, i. 179.
[13] Hubbard, p. 204.
[14] Bradford, p. 310.
[15] Winthrop, i. 352, 353, 369.
[16] Ibid. 145, 180.
[17] Hubbard, p. 205.
[18] Winthrop, i. 188.
[19] Ibid. 63, 180.
[20] Ibid. 195.
[21] Ibid. 198, 204.
[22] Hubbard, p. 207.
[23] Ibid.
[24] "Winthrop, i. 145.
[25] Palfrey, i. 414; Ellis's Puritan Age, pp. 267-291; Dexter's As to Roger Williams, p. 79.
[26] Cotton's Reply to Mr. Williams his Examination, p. 30.
[27] Winthrop, i. 188, 189.
[28] Ibid. 190.
[29] Colonial Records, i. 149.
[30] Winthrop, i. 157-159.
[31] Ibid. 162.
[32] Ibid. 166-169.
[33] As being, perhaps, a too nearly interested party in the issue. One is reminded, however, of a certain nervousness which seems at times to have overborne Mr. Hooker, of which an instance is recorded later, May, 1639.
[34] General History, pp. 305, 306.
[35] Ibid. 173.
[36] Trumbull, i. 216.
[37] Palfrey, i. 383.
[38] Palfrey, i. 447. See also Doyle's English in America, i. 146, 147, 191.
[39] Rev. R. Stansby to John Wilson, April 17, 1637: 4 Mass. Hist. Coll., vii. 10, II.
[40] Winthrop, i. 169; Hubbard, pp. 165, 166.
[41] Magnalia, i. 393.
[42] Winthrop, i. 133.
[43] Hubbard, p. 182.
[44] Mass. Col. Rec, i. 159.
[45] Winthrop, i. 167.
[46] Trumbull's Connecticut, i. 62,63.
[47] Conn. Col. Rec, i., preface iii, and note, text. p. 1.

Chapter Six - Hooker in Connecticut

Section I - The light of the western churches.

Magnalia, i. 303.

The spot on which the Newtown pilgrims arrived was claimed by three different parties, — the Dutch, the Plymouth Colony, and the Indians. The Dutch had built a fort at the mouth of the "Little River," which here flows into the Connecticut, and laid claim to the surrounding territory. The Plymouth people held that the region belonged to them, and resented the intrusion upon it of Massachusetts emigrants. The matter was made the subject of sharp correspondence between the Massachusetts and Plymouth authorities, [1] especially in connection with the occupancy of the territory in the township of Windsor, next north of Hartford, which was taken possession of by the

Dorchester people, notwithstanding the Plymouth colonists had a trading-house there. The Plymouth people indeed regarded the settlement of the three towns of Windsor, Hartford, and Wethersfield as a trespass upon their territory, — a view which the declinature of the Massachusetts government to unite with Plymouth in erecting a plantation there three years before; its assent that Plymouth do it alone, [2] and the objections made in the General Court to the Kewtown people's removal as being to a place outside of the Massachusetts patent, [3] tended certainly to confirm. The "controversie," Bradford says, "ended, but the unkindnes not so soone forgotten." [4]

The Dutch claims to the territory seem to have been intentionally and deliberately ignored. Not so the Indians'. Agents of the Newtown company were employed to purchase the ground; Rev. Samuel Stone and Elder William Goodwin being the persons designated for the purpose. The territory embraced in this purchase was about coincident with that subsequently known as the township of Hartford. The portions needed for the immediate uses of the little settlement were parcelled out in lots of about two acres each, those of Mr. Haynes, Mr. Hooker, Mr. Stone, and Mr. William Goodwin being side by side on the banks of the Little River, flowing then a sweet and healthful stream through the town.

A church-building — not taking account of a temporary structure soon abandoned and given to Mr. Hooker as a barn — destined for ninety-nine years to serve the religious and political uses of the community was built in what was called Meeting-House Yard, a tract of ground covering a somewhat larger extent than that now known as Old State-House Square. Near to the meeting-house were various other then supposed necessary adjuncts to communitary welfare, — the stocks, the pillory, and the whipping post, as well as the market and the jail. The usual time for putting the first three named of these adjuncts of civilization into use was Lecture-day, when the warnings against wrong-doing uttered in the meeting-house could receive practical illustration just outside. Thus while Mr. Hooker or Mr. Stone was expounding morality in the church-edifice, one might have seen the carrying into effect of some one, among other, of the following sentences: [5] —

"Nicholas Olmsteed... [is] to stand vppon the Pillery at Hartford the next lecture day dureing the time of the lecture. He is to be sett on, a lytle before the begining & to stay thereon a litle after the end."

"Walter Gray, for his misdemeanor in laboring to inueagle the affections of Mr. Hoockers mayde, is to be publiquely corrected the next lecture day."

"Susan Coles, for her rebellious cariedge toward her mistris, is to be sent to the howse of correction and be keept to hard labour & course dyet, to be brought forth the next lecture day to be publiquely corrected, and so to be corrected weekley vntil Order be giuen to the contrary."

Not far distant from the church-edifice was the first burying-ground of the little community. It was soon abandoned however, its stones removed, and even the soil graded away, so that no trace of it has remained for two hundred years.

Some structures like sentinel towers or palisades protected the remoter portions of the village from surprise; while within the appointed precincts the people built their houses, shops, and mills, and repeated again substantially the pioneer experiences they had gone through three years before m their Massachusetts home, only this time with probably more carefulness of provision against danger, as being more isolated from support and deeper in the wilderness.

The original government of the three communities grouped within a few miles along the Connecticut had been a commission appointed by Massachusetts. But this provisional condition of things did not even nominally much survive the year of its creation. The claim to jurisdiction over the territory implied in such an appointment was too doubtful, and the spirit of independence in the three settlements themselves was too strong to allow the continuance of such an arrangement. Accordingly, on the first day of May, 1637, there was held a "Gen'rall Corte att Harteford," [6] — so named in honour of Mr. Stone's birthplace in England, — and formal, local and popular [7] government of the Connecticut plantations was established. The first recorded act of this new constituted popular government was a declaration of "offensiue warr ag't the Pequoitt," and a levy of ninety men to fight them. Hartford was called on for forty-two men, Windsor for thirty, and Wethersfield for eighteen. The occasion was what seemed likely to be a general combination of the Indian tribes for the white men's extirpation. In February previous several men had been killed by the Indians at Saybrook. A little later, three men going down the river in a shallop were mutilated, their bodies cut open and hung on trees by the river-side. In April six men and three women at Wethersfield had been killed, and two girls carried captive. Thirty Connecticut dwellers had lost their lives, some of them with barbaric tortures. No Indian historian has recorded for us the provocations which led these poor savages to their cruel revenges; but whatever their provocation — and some certainly they had [8] — the matter had now perhaps reached a stage too late for anything but war.

At any rate, the white people thought so. Capt. John Mason, of Windsor, commanded the little army; Mr. Stone, the Teacher of the Hartford church, went with the soldiers as their chaplain; and before they started Mr. Hooker, the Pastor, made them an address in which he uttered the encouraging declaration "that the Pequots should be bread for them." [9] A letter of Mr. Hooker to Governor Winthrop, written after the expedition had started and before its result was known, gives a little light on the impelling causes of the war: [10] —

"Though we feele nether the tyme nor our strenght fitt for such a service, yet the Indians here, our frends, werr so importunate with vs to make warr presently, that vnlesse we had attempted to do something, we had delivered our persons vnto contempt of base feare & cowardise, & caused them to turne enemyes agaynst vs. Agaynst our mynds, being constrayned by necessity we have sent out a company taking some Indians for guides with vs."

But that it was not humanitarian sentiment which caused hesitation is plain from what follows: —

"I hope you see a necessity to hasten execution & not to do this work of the Lords revenge slackly."

The story is a familiar one of the courageous attack, May 26, on the Pequot fort eight miles northeast of where is now New London, in which several hundred Indians of both sexes and all ages were killed by sword and bullet and fire in about an hour's time. It was hardly a characteristic piece of church-work, yet it is probable that the victors were nearly to a man church members; and the whole enterprise was apparently backed by perfect faith not alone in its necessity but its propriety. And in celebrating the victory stout John Mason says: [11] —

"It may not be amiss here also to remember Mr. Stone (the famous Teacher of the Church of *Hartford*) who was sent to preach and pray with those who went out in those Engagements against the *Pequots.* He lent his best Assistance and Counsel in the Management of those Designs, and the Night in which the Engagement was, (in the morning of it) I say that Night he was with the Lord alone, wrestling with Him by Faith and Prayer, and surely his Prayers prevailed for a blessing; and in the very Time when our Israel was ingaging with the bloudthirsty Pequots, he was in the Top of the Mount, and so held up his Hand that Israel prevailed."

This, done in self-defence and apparent necessity, is probably quite as justifiable as most of the wars of our ancestors with the Indians; but it a little revolts our feelings to find Mr. Ludlow, the lawyer of the colony, and Mr. Pyncheon, soon to be the author of a book, far in advance of his age, on the "Meritorious Price of our Redemption," carrying to Boston a part of the skin and scalps of the vanquished "Sassacus and his brother, and five other Pequot sachems, who, being fled to the Mohawks for shelter...were by them surprised and slain." [12] Even in that hard age there was one man, Roger Williams, humane enough to say of it: [13] "Those Dead Hands were no pleasing sight...I have alwaies showne Dislike to such dismembering the Dead," — a sentiment the cherishing and utterance of which goes far to offset the estimate of the eccentric man necessarily resulting from the facts mentioned in the last chapter concerning him. And when it is remembered that the very next spring following the slaughter of this Pequot tribe and conveyance of scalps and skins to Boston, the settlements along the river were saved from what threatened to be a fatal famine by the purchase of "so much Corn at reasonable Rates "of the Indians at Deerfield," that the Indians brought down to Hartford and Windsor fifty Canoes laden with Corn at one Time," [14] one wonders whether even then a better use might not have been made of the native proprietors of the soil than shooting and burning them.

This aid from Indian sources, together with the safe arrival of a vessel from Boston bringing the important reinforcement to the colony of Mr. Edward Hopkins and his associates, was made a topic of observation in a

Thanksgiving sermon by Mr. Hooker, on Oct. 4, 1638, from the text i Sam. vii. 12: "Then Samuel took a stone, and set it up between Mizpeh and Shen, and called the name of it Ebenezer, saying, Hitherto hath the Lord helped us." [15] In the course of the sermon Mr. Hooker said: —

"It was a sad, sharp winter with us in these western parts, that many lost their lives, not only cattle, but men. But the Lord delivered us. Men concluded it, many affirmed it, never any vessel came to these parts; but the Lord brought it safe. Nay, if you had heard what a battle of men's tongues there was against it; why, the merchant that brought it, the master that guided it, the passengers that freighted it, it was the Lord, brethren, that brought it, it was the Lord that guided it; and truly, had it not been for the Lord we might have perished. Yea, we might have perished for want; but the Lord sent us, as it were, drink out of the rock and meat from the ravens, — the Indians, that they should bring provision and leave it here; it was the Lord that brought it! That a company of poor men should with a boat fall upon such a place, and then prepare for others coming, — it was the Lord that did it! If anything could have hindered, either by truth or falsehood, to keep men from coming to these parts hitherto, it had been done; but yet, notwithstanding, men's minds informed, their consciences convicted, their hearts persuaded to come and to plant. It is the Lord's doing, because his mercy endureth forever!

"The time unseasonable, the winter hard, the corn grown not, — we could not expect but that the hand of the Lord was gone out against us; and truly, it may be it was so. O, it was because the mercy of the Lord endureth forever, that the Lord hath preserved us, — against the malice of devils, the envy of men, and the perverseness of those which seemed to fear God....Let us, when we have seen the Lord in all, — the Lord in the sending of the ship and we not aware of it, — the Lord in bringing us safe, in giving us provisions...labour to have a heart more near unto Him, more endeared unto Him. In all those dealings of His, every expression of God's providence, it should have a touch or a turn, as it were, upon the soul to draw the heart toward him."

In these extracts Mr. Hooker distinctly indicates his belief — a belief which doubtless his hearers entertained with him — that the authorities in Massachusetts discouraged emigration to Connecticut, and misrepresented the condition of things in the new settlement to deter people from coming. The same view of the attitude of the Massachusetts men comes out in a letter written by Mr. Hooker to Governor Winthrop just about the time this sermon was preached. In this letter [16] Mr. Hooker says: —

"Before I express my observations, I must profess, by way of preface, that what I shall write are not forged imaginations and suppositions coined out of men's conceits, but that which is reported, cried openly, and carried by sea and land: secondly, my aim is not at any person, nor intendment to charge any particular, with you; because it is the common trade, that is driven amongst multitudes with you, and with which the heads and hearts of passengers come loaded hither, and that with grief and wonderment. And the conclusion which is aimed at from these reproaches and practices is this, that we are a forlorn people, not worthy to be succoured with company, and so neither with support.

"I will particularize. If inquiry be, what be the people at Connecticut? the reply is, Alas, poor rash-headed creatures, they rushed into a war with the heathen; and? had not we rescued them, at so many hundred charges, they had been utterly undone. In all which, you know there is not a true sentence: for we did not rush into the war; and the Lord himself did rescue, before friends.

"If, after much search for the settling of people, and nothing suitable found to their desires, but toward Connecticut; if yet then they will needs go from the Bay, go any whither, be anywhere, choose any place, any patent — Narragansett, Plymouth, — only go not to Connecticut. We hear and bear.

"Immediately after winter, because there was likelihood multitudes would come over, and lest any should desire to come hither, then there is a lamentable cry raised, that all their cows at Connecticut are dead, and that I had lost nine and only one left, and that was not likely to live, (when I never had but eight, and they never did better than the last winter.) We hear still, and bear.

"And lest haply some men should be encouraged to come because of my subsistence or continuance here, then the rumour is noised, that I am weary of my station; or if I did know whither to go, or my people what way to take, we would never abide: whereas such impudent forgery is scant found in hell; for I profess I know not a member in my congregation but sits down well apayd with his portion, and for myself, I have said what now I write, if I was to choose, I would be where I am.

"But notwithstanding all this, the matter is not sure, and there is some fear that some men will come toward Connecticut when ships come over; either some have related the nature of the place, or some friends invited them; and therefore care must be taken, and is by this generation, as soon as any ship arrives, that persons haste presently to board them, and when no occasion is offered, or question propounded for Connecticut, then their pity to their countrymen is such that they cannot but speak the truth: Alas, do you think to go to Connecticut? Why, do you long to be undone? If you do not, bless yourself from thence; their upland will bear no corn, their meadows nothing but weeds, and the people are almost all starved. Still we hear, and bear.

"But may be these sudden expressions will be taken as words of course, and therefore vanish away when once spoken. Let it therefore be provided that the innkeepers entertain their guests with invectives against Connecticut, and those are set on with the salt, and go off with the voyder. If any hear and stay, then they be welcomed; but if these reports cannot stop a man's proceeding, from making trial, they look at him as a Turk, or as a man scant worthy to live. Still we hear, and bear.

"I suppose you are not a stranger only in Israel, nor yet usually ignorant of these things, being they are not done in a corner, but in open streets, and not by some frantic, forlorn creatures, or madmen, who know not nor care what they say; but, before the ships can come to anchor, whole boats are presently posted out to salute persons, ordinarily, with such relations. The daily expressions of passengers report these, with much grief of spirit, and wonder such wretched falsehoods should be suffered amongst Christians."

It is altogether probable that there was considerable ground for this impeachment by Mr. Hooker of the attitude of the Massachusetts people toward the new settlements in Connecticut. The coming away had not been without friction, and the views of the Connecticut people as to the proper management of public affairs differed in some important particulars from the views of those who controlled in Massachusetts. Still the reply of Winthrop — of which, however, only an imperfect first draft on the back of another document is preserved [17] — shows that he regarded the representations made by his reverend correspondent as exaggerated and indeed rather suited to make one "a little merrye." He says: —

"You complain of the slanderous & reproachfull speeches of some of ors; they report that yor cattle doe not thrive, that yor ground is barrin &c: these are more like the speeches of a prophet ... I know you trouble not yor thoughts with these things exceept it be for recreation, it is well they have no worse matter to laye to your charge; if they had added that you had kept polluted night assemblys, & worshipped the head of an asse &c: then they had sett on with the weight of the old current stampe.

"Yet if you could shewe us the men that reproached you, we should teache them better manners, than to speake evill of this good land God hath brought us to, & to discourage the hearts of their brethren: only you may beare a little wth the more moderate of them, in regard that one of yors opened the doore to all that have followed & for that they may conceive it as lawfull for them to discourage some with us from forsakinge us to goe to you, as for yors to plott by incouragmts &c. to drawe Mr. Shepherd & his wholl church from us. *Sic fama est.*"

The main topic of this correspondence between Mr. Hooker and Governor Winthrop was not, however, the question of a more or less tangible misrepresentation of the state of things in Connecticut. It had to do with the incipient movements toward a Confederation of the colonies, the first steps toward which seem to have been taken at the time of the synod of the elders and messengers of the churches, called together the year before, in August, 1637, about the theological views of Mrs. Anne Hutchinson. For the sake of preserving, so far as possible, chronological sequence in our narrative, it may be best here, rather than elsewhere, to speak of that synod and its occasion.

The trouble which called for the ecclesiastical council had begun a considerable time previous. Mrs. Hutchinson joined the Boston church on Nov. 2, 1634. At that time some objection was made to the opinions she held and expressed on the voyage over. [18] But she seems to have had in that transaction, as well as in some other of her earlier procedures, the support of Mr. Cotton, who had stood in a pastoral relation to her in England. Her husband is described as being a suitable man for a strongminded woman, — "a man of very mild temper and weak parts, and wholly guided by his wife." [19] She was soon followed to this country by her brother-in-law. Rev. John Wheelwright, whom it was speedily proposed to associate with Mr. Wilson and Mr. Cotton in the care of the Boston church, — a project, however, which failed.

Mrs. Hutchinson was a woman of kind heart, quick wits, and persuasive address. Her visitations of the sick, and ministrations especially in the maternal exigencies of her sex, won for her the affection and sympathy of many. She soon established a kind of weekly conference, or Bible-reading as it would now be called, at which she gathered a large number of women and unfolded her peculiar views, and criticised the ministers with the exception of Mr. Cotton and Mr. Wheelwright.

Her peculiar views were, as Winthrop says, "that the person of the Holy Ghost dwells in a justified person. That no sanctification can help to evidence to us our justification." [20] The language is archaic in modern ears, but the idea is not an unfamiliar one in the religious history of many periods, — that a kind of incarnation of the Divine Spirit exists in every Christian, and that every man's evidence that he is a Christian is an immediate perception of the fact, and not an inference from any improvement of his character. Mrs. Hutchinson's doctrine was that to look to any signs, like love of the truth or the transformation of the conduct, as tokens that a man was a saved man, was to be under a "covenant of works." The "covenant of grace" demanded that every Christian should know he was a saved man by an immediate intuition or disclosure of the fact. These notions, as Winthrop says, had "many branches." They led out into exaggerated ideas of the possibility of present revelations, and into depreciated conceptions of the moral virtues. They prompted naturally to contemptuous estimates of the value of learning in religious matters, and to exalted claims to immediate inspiration. The seed fell into heated soil; the whole community was alive with the excitement. Some were intoxicated with the assurance of personal salvation; some, wanting the declared indispensable illumination, were overwhelmed with despair. One woman of the Boston congregation, long troubled with doubts, was driven to distraction, and threw her child into a well, saying, "now she was sure she should be damned." [21]

The partisans of Mrs. Hutchinson were cheered by the support of the young governor, Henry Vane, and by the supposed sympathy of Mr. Cotton; and they rejoiced in proclaiming themselves the representatives of a peculiarly full and free gospel. They claimed that under the direct enlightenment of the Spirit their women and unlettered men preached better than the "black-coats" taught in the "ninny versity," — a designation whose feminine and Hutchinsonian origin it is impossible to question. The matter divided households, and entered into general politics. The Hutchinsonian party looked coldly on the efforts to assist Connecticut in the Pequot war, alleging that the Massachusetts "officers and soldiers were too much under a covenant of works."

The churches of the entire colony were turmoiled; that of Boston was nearly rent asunder. The pastor, Mr. Wilson, supported by Mr. Winthrop and a few others, were on the one side; Mr. Cotton and a majority of the church were on the other. A meeting of the General Court, in December, 1636, called together the ministers and elders to consider the troubles. [22] Mr. Wilson charged the difficulty on the spread of the new Hutchinsonian opinions; whereupon his church, led by Mr. Cotton, his associate, summoned him to answer for it publicly. [23]

A general Fast was observed on the 19th of January, 1637, in view of the "dissension in the churches" and other evils. Mr. Wheelwright, at the afternoon service in the Boston church, preached a sermon which, in the heated temper of the time, was understood to be an assault on the anti-Hutchinsonian party as "antichrists." [24]

The Court judged him guilty of sedition. The Boston church interposed with a petition in his behalf. The excitement was so great that it was determined to hold the next Court of Election away from Boston, — at Newtown. At that assembly, which was on the 17th of May, — just as the Massachusetts and Connecticut soldiers were drawing near to the Pequot encampment, — matters came near to physical violence. [25] Mr. Wilson, the pastor of the Boston church, climbed a tree in the field where the voters were assembled, and addressed them from among the branches. [26] The whole question of officers for the colony turned on the Hutchinsonian views. The result showed that the sympathizers, though many, were in a minority. Governor Vane lost his election, and soon returned to England.

His defeat and departure removed one strong pillar of the delusion. Cooler counsels began to prevail. A day of humiliation was appointed in the churches for the 24th of July. By the coming of August matters were in a better condition for deliberate consideration. In April previous Mr. Hooker had written to Mr. Shepard, of Newtown, — who, in the October following, was to become his son-in-law, — advising against a council on the Hutchinsonian matters. [27] He wrote also, just about the same time, a sympathetic letter to Governor Winthrop on the position the Governor had taken in the affair: [28] —

"When I first heard of those heavy distractions which have risen so vnexpectedly, I did reioyce from the root of my heart, that the Lord did & hath gratiously kept you from any taynt of those new-coyned conceits. You know my playnnesse: you cannot keepe your comfort, nor an honorable respect in Christ in the hearts of His, more then in keeping close to the truth. You shall have what interest I have in heaven to help you in that work."

But when August came, either he had changed his views about a council, or the state of things had changed; for on the 5th of that month Mr. Hooker and Mr. Stone arrived in the Bay from Connecticut by way of Providence, and "Mr. Ludlow, Mr. Pyncheon, and about twelve more," also arrived by another route, as delegates to the same assembly, bringing with them the Pequot skins and scalps before spoken of. The time till August 30th was spent in preliminary consultations, and the 24th was observed as a day of fasting and prayer.

The synod opened its sessions on the 30th of August. It was composed of all the ministerial elders in the country — about twenty-five in number — and delegates from the churches. Mr. Shepard began the deliberations with a "heavenly prayer." Rev. Peter Bulkley, of Concord, and Mr. Hooker, of Hartford, were chosen Moderators. The sessions continued twenty-two days. As a result of the deliberations a list of eighty-two opinions, more or less intimately connected with the recent controversy, were condemned as "some blasphemous, others erroneous, and all unsafe." [29]

It was further resolved, with special reference to Mrs. Hutchinson's Bible-readings, that though females meeting, "some few together," for prayer and edification might be allowed, yet that "a set assembly...where sixty or more did meet every week, and one woman...took upon her the whole exercise," was "disorderly and without rule." [30]

The synod broke up on the 22d of September, and on the following 26th Mr. Davenport, afterward of New Haven, preached by its appointment a sermon of gratulation and good counsel. The expenses of the delegates at Newtown and in travel from Connecticut were paid at the colonial charge. [31] And so after more than two months' absence, Mr. Hooker and Mr. Stone had a chance to go back to Hartford again.

Poor Mrs. Hutchinson — the enthusiastic, kind-hearted, pious, and erroneous occasion of all these disturbances — was soon after called before the Court for continuing her "disorderly" meetings, and promulgating the opinions which, with less or more accuracy of statement or inference, the synod had condemned. She was awhile committed to Mr. Cotton's care, to be reasoned with by him and Mr. Davenport; and subsequently was brought before the Boston church for trial. The trial was in March, 1638, and was on two successive lecture-days, the 15th and 22nd, and was held "befr all the Elders of other Churches, and the Face of the Country." The "saintly" Thomas Shepard and Mr. Welde, of Roxbury, appeared in the character of prosecutors. It is a melancholy story. [32] The attempt was made to force upon her the avowal of immoral opinions concerning the relations of the sexes, which her reverend accusers declared would "necessarily follow" [33] as consequences from her views concerning the resurrection. But this attempt was vain. With all a pure woman's indignation she repudiated the imputation. "I hould it not ... I abhor that Practise." [34] Surrounded by the adroit dialecticians of the Church and State, Mrs. Hutchinson made a substantial retraction of most, certainly, of the errors imputed to her, but was entangled in a labyrinth of confusions between her "Judgement" and her "Expressions," and particularly as to the time when she had first held and proclaimed her opinions. The church, through the mouth of Pastor Wilson, pronounced sentence of excommunication for her "*Erors*" and "forasmuch as *yow have made a Lye*.'" [35] It is impossible to read this trial without sympathy for the poor hounded woman, who, whatever her extravagances and errors, was put as much at a disadvantage before that tribunal as was ever victim of High Commission or Inquisition. Nor is it possible, either, to wink out of sight the fact that exasperating and disquieting as were her procedures at home, it was largely because of their apprehended effect in the old country that such severity of treatment was accorded to her. Following her sentence of deliverance "up to Sathan," and banishment "as a Leper...owt of the congregation," came, on the 28th of the month, her sentence of banishment from the colony. The exiled woman, whom the eye of modern sympathy follows with regret, soon after became a widow, moved to the Dutch frontier, and was, about six years later, with all her children but one of eight years, killed by the Indians. Her views were erratic, and her procedures in the existing state of things were probably to some real extent dangerous; but it may be hoped and believed that heaven was wide enough for her after all.

Her name, however, continued for many years a name of evil omen in New England; a curious illustration of which fact may come appropriately at this point into our story of Mr. Hooker. Perhaps the only recorded saying of Mr. Hooker's wife, Susannah, is quoted in a letter of her husband's from Hartford, about one of the alleged judgments which, in 1637, befell a near relative of Mrs. Hutchinson's who was "infected with her herisies." Mr. Hooker writes:

"While I was thus musing and thus writing, my study where I was writing and the chamber where my wife was sitting, shook as we thought with an earthquake, by the space of half a quarter of an hour. We both perceived it and presently went down. My maid in the kitchen observed the same. My wife said *it was the devil that was displeased that we confer about this occasion*." [36]

It was said earlier in this chapter that the first movements toward the confederation of the colonies — which was the main topic of the letters between Mr. Winthrop and Mr. Hooker from which quotations were there made — were apparently undertaken at the time of the Hutchinson Synod in Boston. In whose mind the scheme of union first originated it is probably impossible to say. The need of such union arose from the common interests and common perils of the colonies themselves. The Dutch and the Indians drove them together in mutual defence. There is apparently no adequate ground for suggesting [37] a Netherland origin for a union which the necessities of the situation itself adequately explain. Plymouth, whose Netherlandish experiences were greatest, was not even present at the original conference on the matter. [38] As a result of this conference, articles of union were first proposed by Massachusetts, and "drawn probably by Governor Winthrop himself." [39] Connecticut, however, objected to the binding power of a majority-vote of the commissioners as proposed by Massachusetts. A difference of judgment, furthermore, as to what ultimate authority opposing views on points controverted among the colonies should be referred for decision — whether to the people as a whole or to the magistrates only — entered into the debate, and was topic of opposing opinion in the correspondence between Mr. Winthrop and Mr. Hooker, wherein Mr. Hooker took, as usual, the democratic side. But the probable immediate cause of the temporary breaking off of the negotiations for federation was the claim of Massachusetts to jurisdiction over Agawam (Springfield), whose inhabitants had accounted themselves a part of the Connecticut Colony, and had acted with those of Connecticut in establishing the government which followed the expiration of the Massachusetts commission in March, 1637. [40] The plan of union was not however abandoned, but was, as there will be occasion hereafter to notice, prosecuted by the personal endeavours of both the eminent men whose correspondence had disclosed so considerable diversity of opinions, and was ultimately carried into successful accomplishment.

[1] Bradford, pp 338-342.
[2] Winthrop, i. 216.
[3] Ante, p. 84.
[4] Bradford, p. 342; Doyle, i. 207, 208.
[5] Conn. Col. Rec, i. 50, 124.
[6] Conn. Col. Rec, i. 9.
[7] Conn. Hist. Soc. Collections, i, 13, 18: Hooker's letter and Trumbull's note.
[8] Lathrop's Centenary Sermon at West Springfield, 1796, pp. 23, 24.
[9] Mason's Brief History, in Mather's Early History, Drake's ed., p 121.
[10] 4 Mass. Hist. Coll., vi. 388, 389.
[11] Mason's Brief History, in Mather's Early History, Drake's ed., p. 157.
[12] Winthrop, i. 281.
[13] Mass. Hist. Coll., xxxvi. 207.
[14] Drake's Mather's Early New England, p. 158.
[15] The sermon was transcribed by Deacon Matthew Grant, of Windsor, possibly from Mr. Hooker's notes and possibly from shorthand notes of the discourse taken by himself. A portion of his painfully difficult manuscript was copied by Dr. J. H. Trumbull and published in the "Hartford Evening Press," Nov. 28, 1860, from which the extracts given in the text are taken. The broken and ejaculatory character of the rhetoric doubtless indicates the imperfect quality of the reporting.
[16] Transcribed from the Massachusetts archives in the Secretary's office at Boston, by Dr. J. H. Trumbull, and published in the Connecticut Historical Society Collections, i. 1-18, with notes.
[17] Life and Letters of John Winthrop, ii. 421.
[18] Hutchinson, ii. 488, 493, 494.
[19] Winthrop, i. 356.
[20] Winthrop, i. 239.
[21] Ibid. 282.
[22] Winthrop, i. 248.
[23] Ibid. 250.
[24] Winthrop, i. 256. But see as to its real quality, Ellis's Puritan Age, p. 322.
[25] Winthrop, i. 262.
[26] Hutchinson, i. 61, note.
[27] Ibid. 68.
[28] 4 Mass. Hist. Soc. Coll., vi. 389, 390.
[29] Winthrop, i. 284. Some of these condemned opinions, though phrased in antique style, are recognizable enough in their modern masquerading attire to justify the reproduction of a few of them here. —

"4. That those that hee in Christ are not under the law and commands of the Word, as the rule of life."

"20. That to call in question whether God be my deare Father after or upon the commission of some hainous sinnes (as murther, incest &c.) doth prove a man to be in the covenant of works."

"39. The due search and knowledge of the Holy Scripture is not a safe and sure way of finding Christ."

"40. There is a testimony of the Spirit, and voyce unto the soule, meerely immediate, without any respect unto or concurrence with the Word."

"43. The Spirit acts most in the saints when they indeavour least."

"47. The scale of the Spirit is limited onely to the immediate witnesse of the Spirit, and doth never witnesse to any worke of grace, or to any conclusion by a syllogisme."

"56. A man is not effectually converted till he hath full assurance."

"64. A man must take no notice of his sinne, nor of his repentance for his sinne."

"70. Frequency or length of holy duties, or trouble of conscience for neglect thereof, are all signes of one under a covenant of workes."

"72. It is a fundamental! and soule-damning errour to make sanctification an evidence of justification."

"77. Sanctification is so farre from evidencing a good estate that it darkens it rather; and a man may more clearely see Christ when he seeth no sanctification than when he doth: the darker my sanctification is, the brighter is my justification."

[30] Winthrop, i. 286.

[31] Ibid, 288.

[32] See Hutchinson's History, ii., appendix; and Report of Trial of Mrs. Anne Hutchinson, in Proc. Mass. Hist. Soc, 2d series, iv. 159-191.

[33] Report of Trial.

[34] Ibid.

[35] Ibid.

[36] Magnalia, ii. 449.

[37] J. Q. Adams, 3 Mass. Hist. Soc. Coll., ix. 211; Palfrey, i. 323; Doyle, i. 306. If a foreign exemplar, however, must be found for so natural an arrangement, why not refer to the Confederation of Switzerland, vastly older than Holland's, and known, by residence under its protection, by English Puritans for generations."

[38] Winthrop, i. 283, 284.

[39] Conn. Hist. Soc. Coll., i. I, Dr. Trumbull's note.

[40] Conn. Hist. Soc. Coll., i. 13, and Dr. Trumbull's note.

Chapter Six - Hooker in Connecticut, Section II.

Section II. The birthplace of American democracy is Hartford.

Johnston's *Connecticut.* p. 73.

Returned to Hartford after the Hutchinsonian Synod in the autumn of 1637, Pastor Hooker doubtless found the interests of the scarcely yet more than one-year-old settlement demanding his care. The winter following was, as has been seen, a "sad, sharp" one, in which many men and cattle lost their lives. In the opening spring the first steps were taken toward the more permanent meeting-house before referred to, in place of the temporary structure till this time employed for the purpose.

But the chief occurrence which makes this year memorable was the preparation in it for the establishment of that written Constitution of popular government which the first few weeks of the following year were to see formally adopted, and which is not only an instrument of unique and intense interest to all students of democratic institutions, but is in some sense Mr. Hooker's most distinguishing and abiding monument.

The preliminary, motions toward the establishment of this distinctively democratic Constitution are very imperfectly recorded. In a true sense they began in the differences which developed in the Bay government before the Connecticut settlers left that jurisdiction, and which were, as has been pointed out, among the efficient causes of that removal. Any careful student of the early history of the Bay Colony cannot fail to see that there is all through it a constant struggle between the two conflicting principles of aristocracy and democracy, and that the Connecticut secession was but one of its earlier manifestations. It was in the communities afterward emigrating to the river that dissatisfaction with the principle of authority earliest and most distinctly showed itself. In 1631 Watertown had objected to the levying of taxes by the Governor and Assistants without consent of the people. [1] In 1632 Newtown was agitated about the limits of the authority exercised by the Governor, "whether by the patent or otherwise;" and a conference between the Deputy and the Governor in the presence of the leading Elders of the colony was had on the subject. [2] In 1634 the deputy of Dorchester to the General Court was disabled from bearing office for three years for denying the magisterial authority of the Governor and Assistants. [3]

The Massachusetts government was not, and was never intended to be, democratic. Its chief civil administrator — a man of the largest nobility and purity of character — had much of the predisposition toward the established in religion and politics characteristic of most men of family and position in his time; and its chief religious representative and counsellor affirmed: "Democracy I do not conceive that ever God did ordain as a fit government either for Church or Commonwealth."

How the company who were associated with Mr. Hooker in his temporary Newtown residence felt on the questions at issue between magisterial and popular rights, was significantly indicated by the fact that when, in 1634, the Assistants voted negatively on Newtown's petition for removal, and the Deputies voted affirmatively, and dispute arose about the effect of the vote, the Newtown people took the vote of the lower house as granting all necessary authority, and made no further application for leave.

What Mr. Hooker's own personal position on the general question of the rights of magistrates and people was, cannot be open to question. An early chronicler says: "After Mr. Hooker's coming over it was observed that many of the freemen grew to be very jealous of their liberties." [4] And this jealousy for popular liberty which his Massachusetts associates must have observed in him and borrowed encouragement from, found in this year of the preliminary procedures for the establishment of the Connecticut Constitution two most signal manifestations.

In the correspondence with Mr. Winthrop, written in the autumn of 1638, Mr. Hooker in the plainest terms avows his broadly democratic sentiments. Mr. Winthrop had written: [5] —

"I expostulated [with Mr. Hooker] about the unwarrantableness and unsafeness of referring matter of counsel or judicature to the body of the people, quia the best part is always the least, and of that best part the wiser part is always the lesser. The old law was, choose ye out judges, etc., and thou shalt bring the matter before the judge, etc."

Whether, as Governor Winthrop's distinguished descendant and biographer contends, [6] this statement of the Governor's views referred "only to matters of 'counsel or judicature,' which not even the democracy of our own days would willingly submit to the 'body of the people,'" or not, Mr. Hooker certainly seems to have taken it in a broader sense. He replied: [7] —

"I fully assent to those staple principles which you set down; to wit, that the people should choose some from amongst them — that they should refer matter of counsel to their counsellors, matter of judicature to their judges: only, the question here grows — what rule the judge must have to judge by; secondly who those counsellors must be.

"That in the matter which is referred to the judge, the sentence should lie in his breast, or be left to his discretion according to which he should go, I am afraid it is a course which wants both safety and warrant. I must confess, I ever looked at it as a way which leads directly to tyranny, and so to confusion, and must plainly profess, if it was in my liberty, I should choose neither to live nor leave my posterity under such a government. Sit liber judex, as the lawyers speak. 17 Deut, 10, 11 — Thou shalt observe to do according to all that they inform, according to the *sentence of the Law.* Thou shalt seek the Law at his mouth: not ask what his discretion allows, but what the Law requires. And therefore the Apostles, when the rulers and high priest passed sentence against their preaching, as prejudicial to the State, the Apostle Peter made it not dainty to profess and practice contrary to their charge, because their sentence was contrary to law, though they might have pretended discretion and depth of wisdom and policy in their charge....

"Its also a truth that counsel should be sought from counsellors; but the question yet is, who those should be. Reserving smaller matters which fall in occasionally in common course, to a lower counsel, in matters of greater consequence, which concern the common good, a general counsel chosen by all, I conceive, under favour, most suitable to rule and most safe for relief of the whole. This was the practice of the Jewish Church, directed by God, Deut. 17: 10, 11; 2 Chron., 19; and the approved experience of the best ordered States give in evidence this way."

It has been well said by a late historian of Connecticut, that this "letter to Winthrop might be made the foundation of the claim that he [Mr. Hooker] had supplied the spirit of the Connecticut Constitution." [8] Its definite formulation of the demand for some rule of determination in civil matters above the "discretion of the magistrates," which the people in Massachusetts had asked for, but found "most of the magistrates and some of the elders not to be very forward" [9] about; and its preference of the counsel of the whole people rather than the advice of "the ministers of the churches," as Mr. Cotton contended for, [10] and Mr. Winthrop practised, [11] mark very clearly the lines on which the Constitution was framed, and fairly indicate the principles which that document, for the first time in human history, put into statutory form.

But Mr. Hooker's title to be regarded as the father of the Connecticut Constitution does not rest on any inference from his general position or from sentiments expressed in a letter like the one above quoted. It has very direct and conclusive support from another source, — support so direct and conclusive that it is regarded as altogether demonstrative by all late writers who have had occasion to notice and estimate its significance.

For the discovery of this interesting fact, not only in Mr. Hooker's story but in the story of constitutional history generally, indebtedness is due to the distinguished antiquarian scholar. Dr. J. Hammond Trumbull, of Hartford; to whom obligation is owing also for the discovery and identification, in its misplaced position in the Massachusetts archives, of the letter of Mr. Hooker repeatedly quoted from above. In this case Dr. Trumbull had a harder and a still more rewarding task. The evidence lay nearly two and a quarter centuries, undeciphered and unconjectured, in a little manuscript book which belonged to Mr. Henry Wolcott, Jr., of Windsor, now in the possession of the Connecticut Historical Society; and of which Dr. Trumbull says, [12] —

"This volume, of about five inches long by four wide, contains 380 pages, closely written, in cipher, — comprising notes of sermons and lectures by Mr. Warham and Mr. Huit of Windsor, and Mr. Hooker and Mr. Stone at Hartford, from April 19, 1638, to April 29, 1641, in regular course. These notes give the dates, texts, and general outline of each discourse; and the questions discussed at the meetings for conference and for catechising, &c. The alphabet made use of is nearly the same with that of Willis (published in 1607), but the great number and variety of arbitrary signs introduced by the writer make the task of deciphering a difficult one."

The sermon in which we are particularly interested was preached by Mr. Hooker at an adjourned session of the General Court of April, 1638. "To this Court, undoubtedly," Dr. Trumbull says, [13] "though the records are silent on this point, was intrusted the formation of the first Constitution, which was formally adopted in January, 1639. Mr. Hooker's sermon, or rather lecture, was delivered on Thursday, May 31, 1638, at an adjourned session, probably, of the April Court, and was apparently designed to lead the way to the general recognition of the great truths which were soon to be successfully incorporated in the Fundamental Laws."

This interesting and important utterance in constitutional history is given, in all that remains of it, here: [14]

"*Text:* Deut. 1: 13. 'Take you wise men, and understanding, and known among your tribes, and I will make them rulers over you.' Captains over thousands, and captains over hundreds — over fifties — over tens, &c.

"*Doctrine.* I. That the choice of public magistrates belongs unto the people by Gods own allowance.

"II. The privilege of election, which belongs to the people, therefore must not be exercised according to their humors, but according to the blessed will and law of God.

"III. They who have the power to appoint officers and magistrates, it is in their power, also, to set the bounds and limitations of the power and place unto which they call them.

"*Reasons.* i. Because the foundation of authority is laid, firstly, in the free consent of the people.

"2. Because, by a free choice, the hearts of the people will be more inclined to the love of the persons [chosen] and more ready to yield [obedience.]

"3. Because of that duty and engagement of the people.

"*Uses.* The lesson taught is threefold:

"1st There is matter of thankful acknowledgement, in the [appreciation] of God's faithfulness toward us, and the permission of these measures that God doth command and vouchsafe.

«2nd. Of reproof — to dash the conceits of all those that shall oppose it.

"3rd. Of exhortation — to persuade us, as God hath given us liberty, to *take* it.

"And lastly — as God hath spared our lives, and given them in liberty, so to seek the guidance of God, and to choose *in* God and *for* God."

Such is the meagre outline, written by an occasional hearer's hand, of a discourse preached before an elected assembly of legislators charged with the business of framing a body of laws for a new commonwealth. It was a discourse preached by the recognized; leader of the colony, by a man of profound scholarship and of persuasive pulpit eloquence measured by the standards of the universities and churches of the home land. It was a discourse which, meagre as it is in outline, was probably elaborated at great length under every head, and may have taken an hour or two hours in delivery. Can any one question the effect of those novel propositions on the minds of those men in the wilderness setting up the fabric of a new popular government? Can any one read those clear definitions of the source, the limitations, and the warrant of all authority in human government, and not recognize the formulation of a new principle in political science? Can any one put this brief document beside the body of Fundamental Laws which this legislative assembly a few months later promulgated, and not recognize from whose far-seeing mind the inspiration and distinctive character of those laws came forth? The evidence is too plain for question. Whose hand soever may in detail have phrased and formulated the Fundamental Laws, — and Haynes and Ludlow and other men there were who might have done it, — the outline of principle and idea, the inspiration and spirit of them, were Thomas Hooker's. It is impossible not to recognize the illuminating mind and guiding will. The pastor of the Hartford church was Connecticut's great legislator also.

And this fact has been recognized by those who have most carefully investigated the evidence. Dr. Leonard Bacon says: [15] —

"That sermon by Thomas Hooker from the pulpit of the First Church in Hartford, is the earliest known suggestion of a fundamental law, enacted not by royal charter, nor by concession from any previously existing government, but by the people themselves, — a primary and supreme law by which the government is constituted, and which not only provides for the free choice of magistrates by the people, but also 'sets the bounds and limitations of the power and place to which' each magistrate is called."

To the same effect is the utterance of Professor Alexander Johnston: [16]

"Here is the first practical assertion of the right of the people not only to choose but to limit the powers of their rulers, an assertion which lies at the foundation of the American system. There is no reference to ' dread sovereign,' no reservation of deference to any class, not even to the class to which the speaker himself belonged. Each individual was to exercise his rights 'according to the blessed will and law of God,' but he was to be responsible to God alone for his fulfillment of the obligation. The whole contains the germ of the idea of the Commonwealth, and it was developed by his hearers into the Constitution of 1639. It is on the banks of the Connecticut, under the mighty preaching of Thomas Hooker, and in the Constitution to which he gave life, if not form, that we draw the first breath of that atmosphere which is now so familiar to us."

So, also, John Fiske says of the Connecticut Constitution of 1639: [17]

"It was the first written Constitution known to history that created a government, and it marked the beginnings of American democracy, of which Thomas Hooker deserves more than any other man to be called the father. The government of the United States to-day is in lineal descent more nearly related to that of Connecticut than to that of any other of the thirteen colonies."

And similarly, in his admirable address at the two hundred and fiftieth anniversary of the adoption of the Connecticut Constitution, Rev. Joseph Twichell says of this utterance of Mr. Hooker: —

"In so few and such words did young Mr. Wolcott of Windsor set down the substance of that great manifesto of liberty; how little deeming that his jottings are the sole record by which more than two centuries later it shall be redeemed from oblivion, and laurel with new and imperishable honor the memory of the divine and statesman who gave it voice."

In the May following the adoption of the Constitution in January, 1639, Mr. Hooker and Mr. Haynes, the governor of Connecticut, went to Boston "and staid near a month." It was during this visit to the Bay that the curious personal incident occurred, illustrative, perhaps, of a certain trait of Mr. Hooker's temperament alluded to before, [18] and illustrative certainly, as a late commentator on the original record which presences the incident for us remarks, [19] of the "inordinate length" — judged by modern standards — "of Mr. Hooker's sermons." The story as Governor Winthrop gives it is as follows: [20]

"Mr. Hooker being to preach at Cambridge, the governour and many others went to hear him, (though the governour did very seldom go from his own congregation upon the Lord's day). He preached in the afternoon, and having gone on, with much strength of voice and intention of spirit, about quarter of an hour, he was at a stand, and told the people, that God had deprived him both of his strength and matter, etc., and so went forth, and about half an hour after returned again, and went on to very good purpose about two hours."

The object of Mr. Hooker's and Governor Haynes's visit to the Bay at this time was the renewal of negotiations about the Confederation which had been unsuccessfully begun two years before. They were moved thereto by increasing apprehension of their Dutch neighbours, "who had lately received a new governor," William Kieft, — an abler man than his predecessor, "who did complain much of the injury done to them at Connecticut." [21] Some agreement or "treaty" appears to have been successfully made or "renewed" [22] between the Massachusetts and Connecticut negotiators; but the formal ratification of a Confederacy, which was the thing Hooker and Haynes desired, was destined still awhile to delay. It came soon, however, hastened at last not only by the increasing vigour of the Dutch administration on the west, but by the breaking out of civil war in England.

The long conflict of Puritanism and Prerogative on the home soil had at last come to the arbitrament of arms. No one could say how it would eventuate. But every consideration impelled the communities which were in substantial agreement with the Puritan party in the conflict, on this side of the water, to draw closer together and be ready for whatever might happen. Accordingly, at the September session of the General Court of Massachusetts, in 1642, "propositions sent from Connecticut about a combination" were referred to a committee, who amended them, and sent "them back to Connecticut to be considered upon against the spring, for winter was now approaching, and there could be no meeting before." [23] The year following, 1643, saw the important enterprise consummated by the agreement of commissioners of the various colonies in twelve articles, which constituted in effect, for certain matters of common interest, a federal government under the title of the "United Colonies of New England." [24]

Mr. Hooker's satisfaction in this long-desired result, and his hearty acknowledgment of the commanding influence in securing its final attainment of the large-minded governor of Massachusetts, from whom he had sometimes differed in judgment on other matters, is well expressed in the following beautiful letter: [25] —

To his much Honored freind John Wyntropp Esquier, Governor of the plantations in the Matcheshusets Bay, dd.

Much Honored in Our Blessed Saviour, — At the returne of our Magistrates, when I vnderstood the gratious & desired successe of ther indeavor, and by the ioynt relation of them all, not only your christian readines, but enlarged faythfullnes in an especiall manner to promote so good a work; though the appearance of flattery (if I know myself & be knowne to you) be not only crosse to my conscience but to my disposition, yet my heart would not suffer me but as vnfeynedly to acknowledge the Lords goodnes, so affectionately to remember your candid & cordiall cariage in a matter of so great consequence; laboring by your speciall prudence to settle a foundation of safety and prosperity in succeeding ages: a work which will be found not only for your comfort, but for your crowne at the great day of your account. Its the greatest good that can befall a man in this world, to be an instrument vnder God to do a great deale of good. To be the repayrer of the breach, was of old counted matter of highest prayse & acceptance with God & man: much more to be a meanes, not only to mayntayne peace & truth in your dayes, but to leave both, as a legacy to those that come after, vntill the coming of the Sonne of God in the clouds.

I know my place & I would not abuse your pacience, or hynder greater imployments: my ayme is nakedly this; to be in the number, & to have my voyce with those, that whyle your self and your faythfull Assistants (as Zerubbabell & his fellow helpers) be laying the first stone of the foundation of this combynation of peace, I may crye grace, grace to your irideavors. And by presenting the worth and acceptableness of the work before you, to strengthen your hands, & encorage your hearts to proceed on with blessing & successe. Goe on therefore (worthy Sir) & be ever enlarged in such worthy services, &: the God of truth & peace will ever be with you, which he desires dayly to begg, who desires to be

Yours in all due respect

Tho: Hooker:

The 15th of the 5th mon: 1643: [26] Sea-Brooke:

This important measure of Confederation, though deficient in its power to reach individual citizenship, or effectually to carry out the legislation of the Union, — much in the same way that the Confederation of the States was deficient a hundred and forty years later, — was nevertheless the most important political step yet taken by the colonies. It could not have been effected even a few years before under the watchful eye of Laud and his Privy Council, who had the government of English colonial affairs in their keeping. But Laud was now in prison. The king was an exile from his own capital. The time was opportune for the establishment of a union which had great immediate practical benefits as well as large educative power in training the scattered colonists of the little New England Commonwealths into mutual trust and confidence. It was also, though they knew it not, a prophecy and forerunner of a greater Confederacy to come, which was to unite the whole Atlantic seaboard settlements into one similar combination, and prepare the way for the federal union of the United States of America.

[1] Winthrop, i. 84.
[2] Ibid. 98-104.
[3] Ibid. 185, 186, and Col. Rec, i. 135, 136.
[4] Hubbard's General History, p. 165.
[5] Winthrop, ii. 428.
[6] Robert C. Winthrop's Life and Letters of John Winthrop, ii. 237.
[7] Conn. Hist. Soc. Coll., i. 11, 12.
[8] Alexander Johnston's Connecticut, p. 71. See, also, Fiske's Beginnings of New England, p. 124.
[9] Winthrop, i. 3S8, 389.
[10] Ibid. 283.
[11] Ibid. 300.
[12] Conn. Hist. Soc. Coll., 1. 19.

[13] Ibid. 19, 20.
[14] Conn. Hist. Soc. Coll., i. 20, 21.
[15] Centennial Conference address, pp. 152, 153.
[16] Connecticut, p. 72.
[17] Beginnings of New England, pp. 127, 128
[18] Ante, p. 85 and note.
[19] Life and Letters of John Winthrop, ii. 244.
[20] Winthrop, i. 366.
[21] Ibid. i. 360.
[22] Ibid.
[23] Winthrop, ii. 102, 103. Cf. Mass. Coll. Rec., ii. 16, 31,
[24] Winthrop, ii. 121, 127.
[25] Life and Letters of John Winthrop, ii. 310, 311.
[26] This date is printed in the "Life and Letters of John Winthrop," and in the Massachusetts Historical Society's republication of this letter, as 1642; but the internal evidence of the letter itself, as well as the distinct indorsement of it by Governor Winthrop as "Rec: (5) 24, 1643," settles its proper date; and as Mr. Robert C. Winthrop, Jr., says in a recent letter to the writer, justifies us in "assuming that Hooker either carelessly made his 3 to look like a 2, or absent-mindedly wrote 2 for 3." See also Proceedings Mass. Hist. Society, May, 1891.

Chapter Six - Hooker in Connecticut. Section III.

Section III.

If any to this Platform can reply
With better reason, let this volume die:
But better argument if none can give,
Then Thomas Hookers Policy *shall live.*

Samuel Stone's *Elegy.*

The turmoiled condition of affairs in England was felt in New England in relation to other than political matters only. The ecclesiastical ground-swell in the home-land had its answering motions here. Puritanism had been taking possession more and more of the popular mind in the old country, and with the assembling of the Long Parliament in 1640 the downfall of the hierarchical system, whose arbitrary administration by Laud had been the main cause of the population of the new settlements in America, was assured.

But the course of Puritanism in England and in New England had been different. In England the progress of dissent from the Establishment had taken main direction toward Presbyterianism. In New England it had been almost exclusively toward Independency. The churches of the new settlements modelled themselves more or less intentionally after that of Plymouth and of the exiles who had brought Congregationalism over with them from Scrooby and Leyden.

This adoption of principles of ecclesiastical procedure divergent to some considerable extent from those of the majority who in England were generally sympathetic with the American colonists in their Puritan views, had been the occasion already of much correspondence between the leading men of the Puritan party there and here. In 1636 or 1637 "many ministers in Old England" sent inquiries to their "Reverend Brethren in New-England concerning Nine Positions" supposed to be taken by the churches of the New England colonies on important points of ecclesiastical usage. This inquiry was followed up in 1638 or 1639 by "two and thirty Questions" of similar character from the same source. Answers to these interrogations were forwarded, — to the first by Rev. John Davenport, of New Haven, and to the second by Rev. Richard Mather, of Dorchester.

The points covered by these inquiries and answers embraced the whole scope of church organization, terms of membership, fellowship with English parishes, office and responsibility of the ministry, power of the laity, doctrinal standards, and authority of councils. It was in reference to the last point — the authority of councils, or synods, as they were then commonly called — that divergence of views here and in English Puritanism most loudly manifested itself, though there was perhaps almost equal difference of judgment concerning the right of each church to institute its own ministry.

But as the conflict in England between the king and Parliament progressed, the tendency of English Puritanism toward Presbyterianism strengthened. It was deemed best to secure the aid of an ecclesiastical synod to settle the religious order of things on that basis. As early as 1641 the London ministers proposed to Parliament the calling of an Assembly, and in December of that year the Commons mentioned the matter as one of their desires in the Grand Remonstrance. [1] A bill was passed for the purpose in 1642, but failed for want of the royal assent. The final order for it, without the king's concurrence, was June 12, 1643. The king, by proclamation, forbade the meeting, and threatened to deprive of their livings those who disobeyed. This substantially prevented the "loyal" portion of the Episcopalians from attending, and added to the certainty of the Presbyterian character of the result.

But an Assembly being determined on, the American divines were not forgotten. A letter from the Earl of Warwick, — Mr. Hooker's old Chelmsford friend and protector, — Lord Say and Sele, Oliver Cromwell, and some thirty other minority members of Parliament, "who stood for the independency of churches," was sent to New England, inviting Mr. Cotton, Mr. Hooker, and Mr. Davenport to "assist in the synod there appointed to consider and advise about the settling of church government." [2] Mr. Cotton and Mr. Davenport were inclined to go; the former the more because in the course of his Scripture expositions at that time he happened to come upon a passage in the Acts which "led him to deliver that doctrine of the interest all churches have in each other's members for mutual helpfulness." Mr. Hooker, with characteristic sagacity, saw the possible complications that might arise from participation in a synod where the views of the New England churches were certain of rejection; and he sent word by the messengers who came on from Boston with the invitation that he "liked not the business, nor thought it any sufficient call for them to go 3000 miles to agree with three men." [3] The "three men" in the Assembly who "stood for independency" were in fact five from the outset, — Thomas Goodwin, Philip Nye, Jeremiah Burroughs, William Bridge, and Sydrach Simpson. As the sessions went on, their numbers doubled; but they were in a hopeless minority.

The wisdom of Mr. Hooker's judgment was soon affirmed by letters from Hugh Peter and others "out of England," advising the invited American divines "to stay till they heard further; so this care came to an end." [4] This assembly, which has passed into history as the Westminster Assembly, was preponderantly Presbyterian; and that party grew stronger in it as its eleven hundred and sixty-three sessions advanced.

This growing, though temporary, dominance of Presbyterianism in England was not without its effect in this country. It gave new vigour and encouragement to a few ministers in the Massachusetts Colony, whose views were more in accordance with that polity than with the Congregational Way around them. The two excellent ministers of Newbury — Thomas Parker, the Pastor, and James Noyes, the Teacher — strongly sympathized with most of the Presbyterian principles; and their church was much disquieted by their advocacy of them. [5]

Fearful of the spread of these dissensions, it was deemed best to hold a meeting of the ministers of the churches at Cambridge to emphasize Congregational principles. This assembly, sometimes erroneously called a synod, — which character, however, it lacked, being a meeting of ministers only, and these non-delegated in their gathering, [6] — met in September, 1643, and was composed of "all the elders in the country, (about 50 in all,) such of the ruling elders as would were present also, but none else." [7]

Here, again, as in the Hutchinsonian Council, Mr. Hooker was one of the moderators; his associate at this time being Mr. Cotton. "They sat in the college, and had their diet there after the manner of scholar's commons, but somewhat better, yet so ordered as it came not to above sixpence the meal for a person...The assembly concluded against some parts of the presbyterial way, and the Newbury ministers took time to consider the arguments." [8]

Consideration of the "arguments" was a chief part of the industry of the time on both sides of the Atlantic. A musketry-fire of pamphlets and a heavier cannonade of bulkier volumes answered one another on both sides of the controversy and of the sea. Two or three lesser tractates by Mr. Cotton, published in 1641 and 1642, were followed about the latter date by the circulation in manuscript form of his "Way of the Churches of Christ in New England." To these was added, from the same ever-ready pen, in 1644, Mr. Cotton's celebrated treatise on the "Keyes of the Kingdom of Heaven." This was at once introduced to the English public by Thomas Goodwin and Philip Nye — members of the Westminster Assembly then in session — as setting forth that "very Middle-way...between that which is called Brownisme and the Presbyteriall-government "which they had contended for in the Assembly. [9] To such of these American tractates as were extant at the time of his writing. Professor Samuel Rutherford, also a member of the Assembly, — and according to John Cotton a "chief Part" of it, — undertook a reply from the Presbyterian point of view. He directed his answer mainly against Cotton's "Way;" Mather's Reply to the "XXXII Questions; "Mather's answer to Herle; and certain treatises of John Robinson's. Mr. Rutherford was an able, courteous, and learned man, and one of the great lights of the Scottish church. He was familiar with a wide range of the literature of the controversy, and was the most competent man of the Presbyterian party to put the argument for that polity into cogent as well as conciliatory form. His book of nearly eight hundred pages, entitled "The Due right of Presbyteries," [10] and a volume by Rev. John Paget, "A Defence of Church Government exercised in Presbyteriall, Classicall & Synodical Assemblies," were deemed by our New England Congregationalists deserving of answer; and notwithstanding Cotton's "Keyes" came out about contemporaneously with Rutherford's volume, a more explicit rejoinder to the Presbyterian treatises was deemed expedient. The task of replying to Rutherford appears to have been assigned to Mr. Hooker, and the answer to Paget to Mr. Davenport. The result of this partition of labor was the production of the two volumes, — Davenport's "Power of Congregational Churches," and Mr. Hooker's "Survey of the Summe of Church-Discipline."

These books had a curious history. At a meeting held at Cambridge, July 1, 1645, "the elders of the churches through all the United Colonies...conferred their councils and examined the writings which some of them had prepared," — these of Hooker and Davenport among the number, — "which being agreed and perfected were sent over into England to be printed." [11]

This is Winthrop's contemporaneous account of what the meeting concluded upon. The books of Hooker and Davenport were not however apparently fully completed, and in point of fact were not sent till the January following. They were then despatched in a vessel sailing from New Haven, which was lost at sea and was never heard of after; save in that spectral phantom of a ship which two years and five months later appeared sailing into New Haven harbor, and which presently, in the sight of a crowd of witnesses, vanished into smoke. This vision Mr. Davenport declared had been given for the quieting of the hearts of those who wondered where the lost vessel and its precious conveyance of passengers had gone. [12]

Convinced of the loss of their manuscripts, the two authors, Hooker and Davenport, re-wrote them; though Hooker his very reluctantly, — as he had indeed reluctantly composed it at the first, — leaving it at last unfinished, to be sent over and printed only after his death. An "Epistle to the Reader," by the hand of his Hartford friends Edward Hopkins and William Goodwin accompanies the reproduced treatise, and explains the circumstances of its origin.

Mr. Hooker's "Survey" is a very able presentation of the early New England view of the church and its administration, as opposed to the Presbyterian conception advocated by his distinguished opponent the Professor of Divinity at St. Andrews, as well as by Samuel Hudson, whose writings are also traversed in Mr. Hooker's reply. The "Survey" suffers, however, in comparison with such a book as the reader easily sees might have been the product of the same pen, by the necessity the author's task seemed to impose upon him, rather to reply to Rutherford in minute detail than to set forth a direct treatise of his own on the subject.

It was perhaps this controversial aspect of the matter which made him so reluctant to undertake the work at first. He says in the Preface of the book, — which from various indications seems to have been also the preface of the book which was lost as well, — "I can professe in a word of truth that against mine own inclination and affection, I was haled by importunity to this so hard a task." And his friends Hopkins and Goodwin remark in their Epistle accompanying the published work: "Some of you are not ignorant with what strength of importunity he was drawn to this *present service,* and with what fear and care he attended it. The weight and difficultie of the work was duly apprehended by him, and he lookt upon it, as somewhat unsuitable to a Pastor, whose head and heart and hands, were full of the imploiments of his proper place." It is matter for regret that the task to which Mr. Hooker was thus "haled by importunity" involved to such an extent the following the track of another's argument, instead of formulating — somewhat after the model of Cotton's "Keyes," for example — a treatise of church polity untrammelled by the necessity of polemic analysis and rejoinder; for that in that case we might have had a document unsurpassed and probably unequalled in clear and vigorous statement of early Congregational principles by any other of New England origin, this treatise as it stands, and especially the Preface, abundantly shows.

In this Preface occurs a kind of summary of the principles set forth in the body of the book. It is a paragraph of importance in more ways than one. It not only gives as succinct a presentation of Congregational principles then entertained as was ever given, but it has the additional interest and value of being a statement of positions concerning which Mr. Hooker says, —

"In all these I have leave to professe the joint judgement of all the Elder's upon the river: Of New-haven, Guilford, Milford, Stratford, Fairfield: *and of most* of the Elders of the Churches in the Bay, *to whom I did send in particular, and did receive approbation from them, under their hands: Of the rest (to whom I could not send) I cannot so affirm; but this I can say, That* at a common meeting [13] *I was desired by them all, to publish what now I do."*

On all grounds, therefore, this brief statement of Congregational principles formulated by Mr. Hooker and assented to by the "elders of the Churches through all the United Colonies," [14] requires a place here.

"*If the Reader* shall demand how far this way of Church-proceeding receives approbation by any common concurrence amongst us: *I shall plainly and punctually expresse my self in a word of truths in these following points,* viz.

Visible Saints are the only true and meet matter, whereof a visible Church should be gathered, and confoe deration is the form.

The Church as *Totum essentiale,* is, and may be, before Officers.

There is no Presbyteriall Church (*i.e.* A Church made up of the Elders of many Congregations appointed Classickwise to rule all those Congregations) in the N.T.

A Church Congregationall is the first subject of the keys.

Each Congregation compleatly constituted of all Officers, hath sufficient power in her self, to exercise the power of the keyes, and all Church discipline, in all the censures thereof.

Ordination is not before election.

There ought to be no ordination of a Minister at large, *Namely, such as should make him Pastour without a People.*

The election of the people hath an instrumental! causal! vertue under Christ, to give an outward call unto an Officer.

Ordination is only a solemn installing of an Officer into the Office, unto which he was formerly called.

Children of such, who are members of Congregations, ought only to be baptized.

The consent of the people gives a causal! vertue to the compleating of the sentence of excommunication.

Whilst the Church remains a true Church of Christ, it doth not loose this power, nor can it lawfully be taken away.

Consociation of Churches should be used, as occasion doth require.

Such consociations and Synods have allowance to counsel! and admonish other Churches, as the case may require.

And if they grow obstinate in errour or sinfull miscarriages, they should renounce the right hand of fellowship with them.

But they have no power to excommunicate.

Nor do their constitutions binde formalitèr & juridicè."

The elaborate volume from whose preface the above extract is quoted was finally published in 1648, and remains a monument of its author's most remarkable learning and great dialectic skill. The first two of the Parts into which the treatise is divided — "Ecclesiastical! Policie Defined," and "The Church considered as it is *corpus Organicum*" — are wrought out probably with about the fulness of the copy lost at sea. The other two — "Of the Government of the Church," and "Concerning Synods," — and especially the latter of them, are wholly incomplete, and would doubtless have been much amplified and illustrated had the author lived to finish the re-writing of his book. The argument, however, is clear throughout, and the subtlety and strength of the presentation of the case for the Congregational Way, as held by the early fathers of New England, entitle the "Survey" to all, at least, of the honour it has ever received as an authoritative exposition of the views in church government which it learnedly and powerfully maintains.

Before the re-writing of the books of Hooker and Davenport was attempted, however, — and indeed perhaps before their authors were perfectly assured of the loss of the first copies made, — the danger of the subversion of the ecclesiastical usages of the colonies seemed so imminent that the Court of Massachusetts, in May, 1646, moved for a general synod, "to discusse, dispute & cleare up by the word of God, such questions of Church governmt & discipline" as had been before spoken of, and others, "as they shall thinke needful & meete;" and invited the ministers and churches of "Plimoth, Connecticott & Newe-Haven," on the same terms of "librty & powr of disputing and voting "as the Massachusetts ministers and messengers. [15] The proposition was received with general acceptance, though with demurrer on the part of the Boston, Salem, and Hingham churches, as a trespass of the civil authority upon the ecclesiastical domain. [16] But most of them finally withdrew opposition, and the 1st of September found all but four of the Massachusetts churches, and a considerable number of those from the other colonies, in session at Cambridge, in what is now called, by way of pre-eminence, the Cambridge Synod, — the best remembered of all the early New England assemblies, and from which the well-known Platform of church polity receives its name. Mr. Hooker, however, was not there. His colleague, Mr. Stone the Teacher, was present, and Deacon Edward Stebbins, a delegate of the church; but the Pastor was absent. He had written his son-in-law, Thomas Shepard, the month before: —

"My yeares and infirmityes grow so fast vpon me, yt wholly disenable me to so long a journey; and because I cannot come myself, I provoke as many elders as I can to lend their help and presence. The Lord Christ be in the midest among you by his guidance and blessing."

Mr. Hooker had made the journey from Hartford to Boston on public business four times certainly, and probably more. [17] It was still a roadless wilderness, to be traversed only on horseback, with a nightly encampment on the ground, under the open skies, by the way. It is not strange that though interested in the synod, he shrank from the repeated pilgrimages.

The synod continued in session at its first gathering only a fortnight. It appointed three of its members to draw up a Scriptural Model of Church-government, and adjourned to June 8 of the following year. Mr. Shepard wrote to his father-in-law, giving account of discussions arising in the synod about the extent of synodical authority, and the power of magistrates in summoning such assemblies. The report received from his correspondent induced the ever democratically-inclined author of the "Survey" to write concerning the first of the two points: —

"I renew thanks for the letter and copy of the passages at the synod. I wish ther be not a misunderstanding of some things by some, or that the bynding power of synods be not pressed too much: for, I speake it only to yourself, he that adventures far in that business will fynd hott and hard work, or else my perspective may fayle, which I confesse it may be."

A comparison of these expressions with the Result [18] of this preliminary session, agreed to "thus far onely, That they should be commended unto more serious consideration against the next Meeting," may perhaps indicate that some jealousy as to synodical authority was justifiable.

On the other point, however, — of the magistrate's power in calling a synod, — Mr. Hooker writes to Shepard: —

"I fynd Mr. Rutherford and Apollonius to give somewhat sparingly to the place of the magistrate, to putt forth power in the calling of synods, wherein I perceive they goe crosse to some of our most serious and iudicious writers."

This implies the same view which Mr. Hooker maintained in his "Survey" on this matter, where he advocates the right of civil authority in summoning ecclesiastical assemblies. Democratic as Mr. Hooker was, he had not, nevertheless, arrived at the modern conception of the separate prerogatives of Church and State; and his doctrines on this matter of magisterial power in ecclesiastical affairs might have been, and probably were, a few years after his death quoted in justification of a long series of meddlesome interferences of the General Court of the colony with the concerns of his own distracted church.

The synod re-assembled, according to adjournment, in June, 1647, but was almost immediately forced to adjourn again by reason of an "epidemical sickness" which prevailed over the whole country among Indians and English, French and Dutch. [19]

Mr. Hooker was one of the victims of the disease. His colleague, Mr. Stone, arrived home from the dispersed synod in season to see him die. He wrote to Mr. Shepard, under date of July 19, 1647: —

Dearest Brother, God brought us safely to Hartford, but when I came hither God presented me a sad spectacle. Mr. Hooker looked like a dying man. God refused to heare our prayers for him, but tooke him from vs July 7 a little before sunne-set. Our sunne is set, our light is eclipsed, our joy is darkened, we remember now in the daye of our calamitie the pleasant things which we enioyed in former times. His spirits & head were so oppressed with the disease that he was not able to expresse much to vs in his sicknesse, but had exprest to Mr. Goodwin before my returne that his peace was made in heaven & had continued 30 years without alteration, he was aboue Satan. Marke the vpright man for the end of that man is peace! He lived a most blameless life. I thinke his greatest enemies cannot charge him. He hath done much work for Christ, & now rests from his labours & his workes follow him, but our losse is great & bitter. My losse is bitter....Mtrs Hooker was taken with the same sicknesse that night when I came to Hartford, & was very neer death, she is yet weak but I hope recouering. It would haue been a great aggravation of our miserie if God had blotted out all that pleasant familee at once. Little Sam: Shepard is well [20] ...

We shall do what we can to prepare Mr. Hookers answer to Rutterford, that it may be sent before winter ... If I have the whole winter you may think whether it be not comely for you & myself & some other elders to make a few verses for Mr. Hooker & inscribe them in the begin? of his book, [21] as if they had been his funeral verses. I do but propound it.

S. Stone. [22]

Mather gathers up and records several more or less authentic incidents of Mr. Hooker's last hours, which may as well be given here as found in the "Magnalia": [23] —

"In the time of his sickness he did not say much to the standers by; but being asked, that he would utter his apprehensions about some important things, especially about the state of *New-England,* he answered*, I have not that work now to do j I have already declared the counsel of the Lord:* and when one that stood weeping by the bedside said unto him. Sir, *you are going to receive the reward of all your labours,* he replied, *Brother, I am going to receive mercy!* At last he closed his own eyes with his own hands, and gently stroaking his own forehead, with a smile in his countenance, he gave a little groan, and so expired his blessed soul into the arms of his *fellow servants,* the *holy angels,* on July 7, 1647."

His age was sixty-one years. He died, it is believed, on the anniversary of his birth. He made a will [24] the day he died, in which he left directions for the guidance of his household and for the custody and publication of his manuscripts; intrusting his "beloued frends, Mr. Edward Hopkins and Mr. William Goodwyn" with the care of the "education and dispose" of his children and the management of his estate.

As was natural, the death of so eminent a leader of the little Commonwealth prompted the remembrance by survivors of portents and supernatural tokens of it. The event occurred in the mid-season of a pestilential summer, when languor and oppression in the probably crowded and ill-ventilated meetinghouse might have been expected. But looking back upon it,

"Some of his most observant hearers observed an astonishing sort of a cloud in his congregation, the last Lord's day of his publick ministry, when he also administred the Lord's Supper among them; and a most unaccountable heaviness and sleepiness, even in the most *watchful christians* of the place, not unlike the drowsiness of the disciples, when our Lord was going to die; for which, one of the elders publickly rebuked them. When those devout people afterwards perceived that this was the last sermon and sacrament wherein they were to have the presence of the *pastor* with them, 't is inexpressible how much they bewailed their unattentiveness unto his *farewel dispensations;* and some of them could enjoy no peace in their own souls, until they had obtained leave of the ciders to confess before the whole congregation with many tears, that inadvertency." [25]

The blow was indeed a great one, and felt not alone in the Connecticut Colony. Some sense of its importance to the whole group of cisatlantic settlements is expressed in the simple, noble language of Governor Winthrop in his account of the pestilence of that disastrous summer: [26] —

"That which made the stroke more sensible and grievous, both to them [of Connecticut] and to all the country, was the death of that faithful servant of the Lord, Mr. Thomas Hooker, pastor of the church in Hartford, who, for piety, prudence, wisdom, zeal, learning, and what else might make him serviceable in the place and time he lived in, might be compared with men of greatest note; and he shall need no other praise: the fruits of his labors in both Englands shall preserve an honorable and happy remembrance of him forever."

This wise and eloquent eulogy, written in the pages of a personal diary with no thought of public reproduction in a biography of the man whom the largehearted Massachusetts governor loved and honoured above all differences which had ever risen between them, needs no amplification.

No portrait or even minute description of Mr. Hooker's physical appearance remains. The impression gained from the various references to him leaves upon the mind, however, the imagination of a figure of dignity and something of command. [27] He is always spoken of by contemporary and by nearly succeeding writers with marked respect and veneration. He is said [28] to have been "a man of a cholerick disposition," which one can easily conjecture from the fervour of his oratorical temperament and the frequent vehemency of his rhetoric. But the same authority which affirms his possession of a fiery spirit says also [29] that "he had ordinarily as much government of his choler, as a man has of a mastiff dog in a chain; he *could let out his dog, and pull in his dog, as he pleased*.'" Eulogiums of his benevolence, of his patience, his humility, as well as of his practical sagacity and wisdom in the management of the affairs of his own and of the neighbouring churches, are preserved on various pages of the pedantic writer to whom, with all his faults and not infrequent inaccuracies, we are indebted for so much that would be otherwise unknown, not only of Hooker, but of most of the fathers of our New England history. One interesting and suggestive illustration of this practical and kindly wisdom in the management of the concerns of his own church must conclude our chapter:

"As for ecclesiastical censures, he was very watchful to prevent all procedures unto them, as far as was consistent with the rules of our Lord; for which cause (except in grosser abominations) when offences happened, he did his utmost, that the notice thereof might be extended no further than it was when they first were laid before him; and having reconciled the offenders with sensible and convenient acknowledgements of their miscarriages, he would let the notice thereof be confined unto such as were aforehand therewith acquainted; and hence there was but one person admonished in, and but one person excommunicated from the church of *Hartford,* in all the fourteen years, that Mr. *Hooker* lived there." [30]

[1] Forster's Grand Remonstrance, pp. 268, 269.
[2] Winthrop, ii. 91, 92.
[3] Ibid.
[4] Ibid.
[5] Coffin's History of Newbury, pp. 72, 115.

[6] See Richard Mather's characterization of it, in his "Reply to Rutherford," pp. 77, 78.
[7] Winthrop, ii. 165.
[8] Winthrop, ii. 165.
[9] "Prefatory Letter" to the "Keyes."
[10] London, 1644.
[11] Winthrop, ii 304.
[12] Bacon's Historical Discourses, p. 107; Atwater's New Haven Colony, pp. 208, 209, and Appendix III. to that volume.
[13] Doubtless the meeting of July 1, 1645, at which the agreement to reply to "many books coming out of England" was entered into at Cambridge.
[14] Winthrop, ii. 304.
[15] Mass. Col. Rec, ii, 155.
[16] Winthrop, ii. 329-332.
[17] In August, 1637; in May, 1639; in September, 1643; and July, 1645. See Winthrop, i. 281, 360; ii, 165, 304.
[18] Result of a Synod at Cambridge in New England, anno 1646, pp. 63-66.
[19] The synod gathered for the third time, August 15, 1648, and after a fortnight's discussion adopted the Platform substantially drafted by one of its three members designated for the purpose at its first meeting, — Rev. Richard Mather, of Dorchester. The principles of the Cambridge Platform are too familiar to need explication here.
[20] Mr. Hooker's grandson by his daughter Susannah, Mr. Shepard's wife.
[21] This was done with more friendship than poetic fire, and verses by Stone, Cotton, and Rogers were printed, with the letter of Hopkins and Goodwin, in the "Survey," which was published in 1648.
[22] 4 Mass. Hist. Coll., viii. 544-546.
[23] Magnalia, i. 317.
[24] Appendix One.
[25] Magnalia, i. 317.
[26] Winthrop, ii. 378.
[27] This impression is well realized in the full-length statue ordered by the State of Connecticut for erection in the State Capitol, a representation of which constitutes the frontispiece of this volume.
[28] Magnalia, i. 313.
[29] Ibid.
[30] Magualia, i. 316, 317.

Chapter Seven - Thomas Hooker's Writings

'T was of *Genevahs* Worthies said, with wonder,
(Those Worthies Three) *Farell* was wont to thunder;
Viret, like Rain, on tender grasse to shower,
But *Calvin,* lively Oracles to pour.

All these in *Hookers* spirit did remain:
A Sonne of Thunder, and a Shower of Rain,
A pourer-forth of lively Oracles,
In saving souls, the summe of miracles.

John Cotton's *Elegy.*

With the single exception of the "Survey of the Summe of Church Discipline," spoken of in the last chapter, Mr. Hooker was not in primary purpose an author of books. Of his published writings some thirty titles are indeed extant. [1] Yet all these volumes, with the exception of the one on Church Polity, to whose composition he had been "haled by importunity," were at first discourses, whose original and main use was oral delivery, and whose chief object was the immediately practical one of impressing, convincing, and persuading the hearers of his voice.

Some of these discourses were apparently printed from notes taken down by hearers of his Lectures at Chelmsford, or possibly still earlier at Emmanuel; and even of others, concerning which we have the assurance that they are "as they were penned under his own hand," or "printed from his own papers written with his own hand," [2] we have no tokens of editorial revision by himself, and little of any intention in their composition that they should be printed at all. All his books — unless "The Poore Doubting Christian" be a possible exception — being published in England, either during his exile in Holland, his residence in America, or after his death, he saw none of them through the press; and though authorizing the issue of some of them, imparted to none the benefit of an author's customary review of the printed page. One of them — "The Saints Dignitie and Dutie," published in 1651 — was compiled by his son-in-law, Shepard; two or three others — as "A Comment upon Christs Last Prayer," published in 1656, and "The Application of Redemption," published in 1659 — were issued under the prefatory supervision of Rev. Thomas Goodwin and Rev. Philip Nye; and some in all probability were printed from copies of Mr. Hooker's discourses made by Rev. John Higginson, of Guilford, who is said [3] to have "transcribed from his manuscripts near two hundred of these excellent sermons which were sent over into *England* that they might be published; but by what means I know not, scarce half of them have seen the light unto this day." Several of the volumes are altogether anonymous, — a fact itself suggestive of the surreptitious use and publication of the materials of which they were compiled.

But though there is some diversity in the details of style and finish, such as this variety of manner in the appearance of the volumes would suggest, the family likeness is unmistakable. They obviously came, whatever verbal blemish may attach to them, from the same mind and pen.

Mr. Hooker was regarded by his associates — themselves men of great learning — as a learned man; and indications of the fact come out distinctly in his "Survey," and, in an exegetical way, to some extent in his discourses. But one looks in vain in his writings, as in the writings of his Puritan contemporaries generally, for any apparent knowledge of current secular literature. The poets of the Elizabethan period find not the slightest token of existence in his pages. Shakspeare died in Hooker's university days; Bacon while he was preaching at Chelmsford; but neither the poetry of the one nor the philosophy of the other, nor the literature which either of them stood in any wise the representative of, apparently came in the least degree within the ken of Hooker, any more than they did within the ken of most of his associates in the Puritan ministry of his time. Even the literature of the Prayer-book, with which they must have been familiar from childhood, is almost unreflected in their pages.

Of the graces of a literary style, therefore, Hooker must not be looked to as an illustrator. He himself says, in the preface to his "Survey," what is applicable to all his writings: —

"As it is beyond my skill, so I professe it is beyond my care to please the nicenesse of men's palates with any | quaintnesse of language. They who covet more sauce then meate, they must provide cooks to their minde...The substance and solidity of the frame is that which pleaseth the builder, it is the painters work to provide varnish."

This disclaimer is in Hooker's genuine style. It is itself an illustration of that homely vigour and vivacity which made his pulpit utterances so arrestive of the most wandering or antagonistic attention, and makes the faded pages of his printed books frequently so lively and picturesque.

As to the mass of his writings, they are — laying aside the "Survey" — essentially on one theme. They are a body, not of doctrinal, but of experimental divinity. The discourses of which they are composed are said to have been, [4] and it is inherently probable that they were, the result of repeated preachings and lecturings upon the experimental aspects of religion, first at Cambridge when he lectured at Emmanuel, afterward at Esher and Chelmsford, and subsequently in America. He went over the ground again and again with marvellous minuteness and fulness of detail. His volumes are, when collected into their organic relationship, a development of what he conceived to be the soul's way of seeking, finding, and enjoying Christ. Their titles, whether his own or given by others, distinctly indicate this recognized purpose running through them. "The Soules Preparation for Christ," "The Soules Humiliation," "The Soules Vocation," "The Soules Justification," "The Soules Implantation," "The Soules Vnion with Christ," "The Soules Benefit from Vnion with Christ," "The Saints Dignitie and Dutie," — these, among others, show clearly the track along which he moved.

It is the line of thought followed rather by the pastor than the theologian. The robustest Calvinistic system of theology is everywhere implied and incidentally expressed in these discourses, but the statement of a system of theology is in none of them, or all of them, an aim. The aim is the persuasion of men; and to this purpose the preacher brings a fecundity of conception, a power of spiritual anatomy, an amplitude and variousness of illustration, and an energy of utterance truly wonderful. Especially striking is this anatomic skill in dealing with the moral phenomena at that time so generally antecedent to, or attendant upon, conversion. To most modern readers the proportion will seem excessive which Mr. Hooker gives to the experiences of the soul in mere "preparation" for conversion. He has volumes on these preliminary exercises of the spirit before it gets to the point of trust in Christ. He laid himself open, even while he lived, to the remark of the shrewd Rev. Nathaniel Ward, of Ipswich: "Mr. Hooker, you make as good Christians before men are in Christ as ever they are after; would I were but as good a Christian now as you make men while they are but preparing for Christ." [5]

Mr. Hooker's course in this respect was probably extreme even for his time. But in those days of recoil from the outward ceremonial religion in which the Papacy had so long held men, the inward facts of personal experience were made the subject of the most careful scrutiny and dissection. Especially all the evasions and windings of the human spirit in recoil from the stern presentations made of the sovereignty and righteousness of God. were followed with microscopic acuteness and pitilessness of exposure. Conversion was a great thing and a difficult thing. It was "not a little mercy that will serve the turne...the Lord will make all crack before thou shalt finde mercy." [6] Mr. Hooker's son-in-law, the "saintly" Thomas Shepard, put the matter thus in his "Sincere Convert": "Jesus Christ is not got with a wet finger. ... It is a tough work, a wonderfull hard matter to be saved." [7] And again: "'T is a thousand to one if ever thou bee one of that small number whom God hath picked out to escape this wrath to come." [8]

Holding these views of the immense difficulty of saving conversion, the vast liability to deception about it, together with the infinite misery of failure in the enterprise, it is not strange that the whole process of the spiritual enterprise should have been tried as by fire. As specimens of this kind of endeavour Hooker's writings are unsurpassed. Of this feature of his teachings, as well as of others which will afford a more general view of his spirit and method as a preacher, the best conception will be gained by some quotations from his books.

In "The Soules Preparation for Christ," the preacher is arguing on the necessity of a clear view of a man's sinfulness, and says: [9] —

"First it is not every sight of sinne will serve the turne, nor every apprehension of a mans vilenesse; but it must have these two properties in it, First, he must see sinne clearely; Secondly, convictingly. First, he that will see sinne clearely, must see it truly and fully, and be able to fadome the compasse of his corruptions, and to dive into the depth of the wretchednesse of his vile heart, otherwise it wil befall a mans sinne as it doth the wound of a mans body: when a man lookes into the wound overly, and doth not search it to the bottome, it begins to fester and rancle, and so in the end he is slaine by it; so it is with most sinners, wee carry it all away with this, Wee are sinners; and such ordinary confessions; but we never see the depth of the wound of sin; and so are slaine by our sinnes. It is not a generall, slight, and confused sight of sinne that will serue the turne: it is not enough to say, It is my infirmity, and I cannot amend it: and wee are all sinners and so forth. No, this is the ground why wee mistake our evils and reforme not our wayes, because we have a slight and overly sight of sinne; a man must prove his wayes as the Goldsmith doth his gold in the fire, a man must search narrowly and have much light to see what the vilenesse of his owne heart is, and to see what his sinnes are, that doe procure the wrath of God against him. ...We must looke on the nature of sinne in the venome of it, the deadly hurtful! nature that it hath for plagues and miseries, it doth procure to our soules; and that you may doe, partly if you compare it with other things, and partly if you looke at it in regard of yourselves: First, compare sinne with those things that are most fearefull and horrible; As suppose any soule here present were to behold the damned in hell, and if the Lord should give thee a httle peepe-hole into hell, that thou didst see the horror of those damned soules, and thy heart begins to shake in consideration thereof; then propound this to thy owne heart, what paines the damned in hell doe endure for sinne, and thy heart will shake and quake at it, the least sinne that ever thou didst commit, though thou makest a light matter of it, is a greater evill then the paines of the damned in hell, setting aside their sinne; all the torments in hell are not so great an evil, as the least sin is: men begin to shrink at this, and loathe to goe down to hell, and to be in endlesse torments."

But such a thorough sight of sin is needful to a thorough work of grace; for [10] —

"Many have gone a great way in the worke of humiliation, and yet because it never went through to the quicke, they have gone backe againe, and become vile as ever they were; I have known men, that tlxe Lord hath layed a heavie burthen upon them, and awakened their consciences, and driven them to a desperate extremity, and yet after much anguish, and many resolutions, and the prizing of Christ, as they conceived, and after the renouncing of all, to take Christ upon his owne termes as they imagined; and even these when they have bin eased and refreshed, and God hath taken off the trouble, they have come to be as crosse to God and all goodnesse, and as full of hatred to Gods children as ever and worse too.

"Now why did these fall away? Why were they never Justified and Sanctified? and why did they never come to beleeve in the Lord Jesus? The reason is, because their hearts were never pierced for their sinne, they were never kindly loosened from it; this is the meaning of that place in ler. Plow up the fallow ground of your hearts, and sowe not among thornes, it is nothing else, but with sound saving sorrow to have the heart pierced with the terrours of the Law seising upon it, and the vilenesse of sin wounding the conscience for it. The heart of man is compared to fallow ground that is unfruitfull; you must not sow amongst thornes and thistles, first plow it, and lay it bare and naked, and then cast in your seed. If a man plow here a furrow, and there a furrow, and leave here and there a bawke, hee is never like to have a good crop, there will grow so many thistles and so much grasse, that it will choake the seed: our hearts are this ground, and our corruptions are these thornes and thistles: Now if a man be content to finde some sinne hatefull, because it is shamefull; but will keepe here a lust and there a lust, hee will never make any good husbandry of the heart: though a faithfull Minister should sow all the grace of promises in his soule, he would never get any good by them, but the corruptions that remaine in the heart will hinder the saving work thereof. Therefore plow up all, and by sound saving sorrow labour to have thy heart burthened for sinne, and estranged from it, and this is good husbandry indeed."

But there is great liability to self-deception about this matter: —

"Oh doe not cozen your owne soules; it is not the teares of the eye, but the blood of the heart that your sinnes must cost, and if you come not to this, never thinke that your sorrow is good....Now if all be true that I have said, there are but few sorrowers for sinne, therefore few saved; here wee see the ground and reason why many fly oif from Godlinesse, and Christianity: This is the cause, their soules were onely troubled with a little hellish sorrow, but their hearts were never kindly grieved for their sinnes. If a mans arme be broken and disjoynted a little, it may grow together againe; But if it be quite broken off, it cannot grow together; so the terrour of the Law affrighted his conscience, and a powerfull Minister unjoynted his soule, and the Judgements of God were rending of him; but he was never cut off altogether: and therefore he returnes as vile, & as base, if not worse then before, & he growes more firmly to his corruptions. It is with a mans conversion, as in some mens ditching; they doe not pull up all the trees by the roots, but plash them: so when you come to have your corruptions cut off, you plash them, and doe not wound your hearts kindly, and you doe not make your soules feele the burthen of sinne truly: this will make a man grow and flourish still, howsoever more cunningly and subtilly...Looke as it is with a womans conception, those births that are hasty, the children are either still borne, or the woman most commonly dies; so doe not thou thinke to fall upon the promise presently. Indeed you cannot fall upon it too soone upon good grounds; but it is impossible that ever a full soule or a haughty heart should beleeve, thou mayest be deceived, but thou canst not be engrafted into Christ: therfore when God begins to worke, never rest till you come to a full measure of this brokennesse of heart. Oh follow the blow and labour to make this worke sound and good unto the bottome." [11]

But one test and measure of this "sound work" inculcated by Hooker has not, perhaps, attracted the notice its place in our American religious history deserves. It is that test of true conversion which in New England theology is commonly connected with the name of Dr. Hopkins, of Newport, — that a Christian should be willing to be damned if it be God's will. Cotton Mather [12] follows his father Increase [13] in an attempt to defend Mr. Hooker from the imputation of teaching this doctrine, on the ground that the publication of Mr. Hooker's writings was to a great extent "without his consent or knowledge; whereby his notions came to be deformedly misrepresented in multitudes of passages, among which I will suppose that crude passage which *Mr. Giles Firmin,* in his *Real Christian* so well confutes, *That if the soul be rightly humbled, it is content to bear the state of damnation.*" The defence is well meant, but it is idle. The Hopkinsian doctrine of contentment in being damned was taught, nearly a century and a half before Hopkins, by Hooker and his son-in-law Shepard with the utmost distinctness. It is not by any supposition of incorrect reporting that the tenet can be got out of Hooker's "Humiliation" or Shepard's "Sincere Convert." Hooker's "Humiliation" is one of the best published of all his treatises, and bears internal evidence of as much accuracy in reproducing his thought and idiom of speech as any other.

And the doctrine in question is logically and rhetorically woven into the texture of both Hooker's and Shepard's volumes. It appears and reappears in them. It is prepared for, led up to, stated, enforced, and objections to it answered. There is no accidental and inconsiderate slipping into its utterance. It is accepted with full intelligence, and with clear recognition of its obnoxiousness and its difficulty to common experience.

The teachings of Hooker and his son-in-law on this matter were made the topic of correspondence between Shepard and Rev. Giles Firmin, and of an elaborate treatise by Firmin, largely in confutation of the utterances of Shepard and his father-in-law on the doctrine in question. [14] Many pages might be quoted from Shepard's writings in support of this doctrine, but attention must here be confined to Hooker's teachings on the subject.

The preacher is well aware he is dealing with a hard point: —

"Now I come to this last passage in this worke of Humiliation, and this is the dead lift of all. The Prodigall doth not stand it out with his Father and say, I am now come againe, if I may have halfe the rule in the Family, I am content to live with you. No, though hee would not stay there before, yet now hee cannot be kept out, hee is content to bee anything...Lord (saith he) shew me mercy, and I am content to be, and to suffer anything. So from hence the Doctrine is this. *The Soule that is truly humbled is content to be disposed by the Ahnightie, as it pleaseth him.* The maine pitch of this point lyes in the word content. This phrase is a higher pitch then the former of submission: and this is plaine by this example. Take a debtor, who hath used all meanes to avoyd the creditor: in the end he seeth that hee cannot avoyd the suit, and to beare it hee is not able. Therefore the onely way is to come in, and yield himselfe into his creditors hands; where there is nothing, the King must loose his right; so the debtor yields himselfe: but suppose the creditor should use him hardly, exact the uttermost, and throw him into the prison; Now to bee content to undergoe the hardest dealing it is a hard matter: this is a further degree then the offering himselfe. So, when the Soule hath offered himselfe, and he seeth that Gods writs are out against him, and his conscience (the Lords Serjeant) is coming to serve a Subpcena on him, and it is not able to avoyd it, nor to beare it when he comes, therefore he submits himselfe and saith. Lord, whither shall I goe, thy anger is heavy and unavoydable; Nay, whatsoever God requires, the Soule layes his hand upon his mouth, and goes away contented and well satisfied, and it hath nothing to say against the Lord. This is the nature of the Doctrine in hand; and for the better opening of it let me discover these things..., For howsoever the Lords worke is secret in other ordinary things, yet all the Soules that ever came to Christ, and that shall ever come to Christ, must have this worke upon them; and it is impossible that faith should be in the Soule; except this worke bee there first, to make way for faith. [15] ...

"Thirdly, Hence the Soule comes to be quiet and framable under the heavy hand of God in that helplesse condition wherein he is; so that the Soule having been thus framed aforehand, it comes to this, that it takes the blow and lies under the burthen, and goes away quietly and patiently, he is quiet and saith not a word more: oh! this is a heart worth gold. He accounts Gods dealing and Gods way to be the fittest and most seasonable of all. Oh (saith he) it is fit that God should glorifie himselfe though I be damned forever, for I deserve the worst. [16] ...

"Now see this blessed frame of heart in these three particulars. First, the Soule is content that mercy shall deny what it will to the Soule, and the Soule is content and calmed with whatsoever mercy denyes. If the Lord will not heare his prayers, and if the Lord will cast him away, because he hath cast away the Lords kindnesse, and if the Lord will leave him in that miserable and damnable condition, which he hath brought himselfe into, by the stubbornnesse of his heart, the Soule is quiet. Though I confesse it is harsh and tedious, and long it is ere the Soule be thus framed; yet the heart truely abased is content to beare the estate of damnation; because hee hath brought this misery and damnation upon himselfe." [17]

"But some may here object and say. Must the Soule, can the Soule, or ought it to be thus content, to be left in this damnable condition? For the answer hereof; Know that this contentednesse implies two things, and it may bee taken in a double sense. First, Contentedness sometimes implies nothing else, but a carnall securitie....But then; Secondly, it implies a calmnesse of the Soule not murmuring against the Lords dispensation toward him. ... So wee should not bee carelesse in using all meanes for our good, but still seeke to God for mercy; yet thus we must be, and thus we ought to be contented with whatsoever mercy shall deny, because wee are not worthy of any favour; and the humble Soule reasons thus with itselfe and saith, my owne sinne, and my abominations have brought me into this damnable condition wherein I am, & I have neglected that mercy which might have brought me from it, therefore why should I murmure against mercy, though it deny me mercy? ...Marke this well. He that is not willing to acknowledge the freenesse of the course of mercy, is not worthy, nay, hee is not fit to receive any mercy; but that Soule which is not content that mercy deny him what it will; he doth not give way to the freenesse of the Lords grace and m.ercy, and therefore that Soule is not fit for mercy. [18] ...

"But some may object. Can a man feele this frame of heart, to be content, that mercy should have him in hell? doe the Saints of God find this? and can any man know this in his heart?

"To this I answer. Many of Gods servants have been driven to this, and have attained to it, and have laid open the simphcitie of their Soules, in being content with this." [19] ...

"The soule that is thus contented to be at Gods disposing, it is ever improving all meanes and helpes that may bring him neerer to God, but if mercy shall deny it, the soule is satisfied and rests well apaid; this every Soule that is truely humbled may have, and hath in some measure." [20]

But this submission and humiliation of the soul no one can accomplish for himself; for —

"This union that is betweene the Soul and its corruptions is marvellous strong and firme, nay so strong and firme that there is no meanes under heaven, no creature in the world that is able to breake this union, and dissolve this combination that is betweene sinne and the soule, unless the Lord by his Almighty power come and break this conspiracy that is betweene sin and the soule against himselfe and the glory of his name... As it is with the body of a man if there were a great and old distemper in a mans stomacke, if a man should put a rich doublet upon him and lay him in a Featherbed and use all other outward meanes this would doe him noe good because the disease is within... lust so it is with the soule of a man; a mans heart will have his sinne; there is an inward combination betweene the soule and sinne; now all meanes, as the Word and the like, is outward, and can doe no good in this kind, they cannot break the union betweene a mans heart and his corruptions, unless the Lord by his Almighty power and infinite wisdome make a separation betweene sinne and the soule, and dissolve this union." [21]

And God does sometimes interpose to afford this indispensable aid. Not always, indeed, for God's purpose does not always go to the extent of a saving work.

"The Lord deales diversely as hee seeth fit; specially in these three wayes. First, if God have a purpose to civilize a man, he will lay his sorrow as a fetter upon him; he onely meanes to civilize him, and knocke off his fingers from base courses... God onely rips the skinne a little, and layeth some small blow upon him: but if a man have beene a rude and a great ryoter, the Lord begins to serve a Writ upon him ... so that now the soule seeth the flashes of hell, and Gods wrath upon the soule, and the terrours of hell lay hold upon the heart, and he confesseth that hee is so, and hee hath done so, and therefore he is a poore damned creature, and then the soule labours to welter it, and it may be his conscience will bee deluded by some carnall Minister that makes the way broader than it is, ...or else it may be, hee stops the mouth of conscience with some outward performances: ...and he wil pray in his family, and heare sermons, & take up some good courses; & thus he takes up a quiet civill course, and stayeth here a while, and at last comes to nothing: And thus God leaves him in the lurch, if he meanes onely to civilize him.

But secondly, if God intends to doe good to a man, hee will not let him goe thus, and fall to a civill course... The Lord will ferret him from his denne, and from his base courses and practises: He will be with you in all your stealing and pilfering, and in all your cursed devices, if you belong to him hee will not give you over... Now the soule is beyond all shift; when it is day, he wisheth it were night, and when it is night, hee wisheth it were day; the wrath of God followeth him wheresoever he goeth, and the soule would fain be rid of this, but hee cannot; and yet all the while the soule is not heavy and sorrowfull for sin; hee is burdened, and could bee content to throw away the punishment and horror of sinne, but not the sweet of sinne: as it is with a child that takes a live coale in his hand, thinking to play with it, when hee feeles fire in it, hee throwes it away; hee doth not throw it away because it is black, but because it burnes him: So it is here: A sinfull wretch will throw away his sinne, because of the wrath of God that is due to him for it, and the drunkard will be drunke no more; but if he might have his queanes and his pots without any punishment or trouble, he would have them with all his heart, hee loves the black and sweet of sinne well enough, but he loves not the plague of sinne... Now in the third place, if the Lord purpose to doe good to the soule, he will not suffer him to be quiet here, but hee openeth the eye of the soule further; and makes him sorrow, not because it is a great and shamefull sinne, but the Lord saith to the soule, Even the least sinne makes a separation betweene mee and thee; and the heart begins to reason thus: Lord, is this true? is this the smart of sinne? and is this the vile nature of sinne? O Lord! how odious are these abominations that cause this evill, and though they had not caused this evill, yet this is worse then the evill; that they make a separation betweene God and my soule. Good Lord, why was I borne?" [22]

So that if God really intends to save a man he does not stop with any "morall and external drawing," but he works "effectually" to that end.

"I expresse it thus, looke as it is with the wheele of a clock, or the wheele of a lack that is turned aside, and by some contrary poyse set the wrong way. He now that will set this wheele right, must take away the contrary poyse, and then put the wheele the right way, and yet the wheele doth not goe all this while of it selfe, but first there is a stopping of the wheele, and a taking away of the poyse: and secondly the wheele must be turned the right way, and all this while the wheele is only a sufferer; so it is with the soule of a man, the heart of a man, and the will of a man, and the affections of a man; they are the wheeles of the soules of men... Now when the Lord commeth to set these wheeles aright, he must take away the poyse and plummet that made them runne the wrong way, that is, the Lord by his almighty power, must overpower those sins and corruptions which harbour in the soule...and then the frame of the soule will be to God-ward, it will be in a right frame and order, it will runne the right way, and all this while the will is only a sufferer, and this I take to be the meaning of the text: That God by a holy kind of violence, rendeth the soule of a poore sinner, and withall by his almighty power, stops the force of a mans corruptions, and makes the soule teachable, and framable to the will of God, it makes it to lie levell, and to be at Gods command, and this is done by a holy kind of violence." [23]

But when this "effectual" sovereign work of grace is accomplished, there is no end to the consolations of the gospel.

"It is a word of consolation, and it is a cordiall to cheare up a mans heart, and carry him through all troubles whatsoever can betide him or shall befall him. This doctrine of Iustification it seems to me to be like *Noahs* Arke, when all the world was to bee drowned: God taught *Noah* to make an arke, and to pitch it about, that no water, nor winds, nor stormes could breake through, and so it bore up *Noah* above the waters, and kept him safe against wind and weather; when one was on the top of a mountain crying: O save me, another clambering upon the trees, all floting, and crying, and dying there; there was no saving but for those only that were gotten into the arke: Oh so it will be with you poor foolish beleevers, the world is like this sea, wherein are many floods of water, many troubles, much persecution: Oh get you into the arke the Lord Jesus, and when one is roring and yelling. Oh the devill, the devill;

another is ready to hang himselfe, or to cut his owne throat; another sends for a Minister, and hee crieth. Oh there is no mercy for mee, I have opposed it; Get you into Christ, I say, and you shall bee safe I will warrant you; your soules shall bee transported with consolation to the end of your hopes." [24]

And of such justified state the Spirit of God gives inward witness: —

"The spirit doth evidence to the soule, broken and humbled. That the soule hath an interest in this mercy, that it was appointed for it, and he hath to meddle with it...We may observe that a witnesse in a cause doth marvellously cleare it, if he be wise and judicious, and the thing that before was doubtfull, comes now to be apparant: as now in a point of Law, two men contend for land; now if an ancient wise man of some place is called before the Judge at the Assizes, and hee beares witnesse upon his knowledge, that such Landes have beene in the possession of such a generation or family, for the space of many yeares; this is a speciall testification, that this man being of that generation, he hath an interest in these lands: So it is with the witnesse of Gods Spirit, there is a controversie betweene Satan and the soule, the soule saith, oh, that grace and compassion might be bestowed on mee; why, (saith Satan) dost thou conceive of any mercy, or grace and Salvation? marke thy rebellions against thy Saviour, marke the wretched distempers of thy heart, and the filthy abhomi nations of thy life: dost thou thinke of mercy? ...Now the Spirit of God comming in, that casts the cause and makes it evident, if such a poore heart have interest, and may meddle and make challenge to mercy and salvation, because it hath beene prepared for them, from the beginning of the world to this very day. Now this gives a light into the businesse, & the evidence is sure, that this man hath title to all the riches and compassion of the Lord Jesus; *Acts.* i. 39. Every poore creature thinkes, that God thinkes so of him, as hee thinkes of himselfe...whereas the Spirit of the Lord judgeth otherwise, and God meanes well toward him, and intends good to all you that have beene broken for your sins; and there is witnesse of it in heaven, and it shall be made good to your owne consciences." [25]

Which gives a good ground for comfort and cheerful living: —

"Come what wil come. This is his aim to settle the conclusion of their happines, and the certainty thereof: To be beyond the reach of al the hosts in Heaven and Earth. Therefore he musters up al, what we are, what shal be. If there were a thousand worlds to come, and should set themselves to shake the comforts of the faithful, it could not be... The Devils and sin may as wel separate Christ from the Father, as pul the love of the Father from his own heart, and so from Christ, as separate us from it... Be therefore content with what thou hast, our Saviors desire is to interest thee in the heart and love of the Father, as himself. Not to love thee as a Creature, as a friend, a subject, but as the Son of his love. What me f Yes thee, poor, weak, silly, worthless Worm, that beleevest in him. Go thy way therefore, never quarel, nor question any more. It is enough, nay it is too much. I would not have thought it. I durst not have desired it. I could not have beleeved it, but that our Savior hath said and done it." [26]

But what sort of preaching is it which leads to these salvatory results? Hooker gives his idea about it in answering the question, "What is a powerful minister?"

"The word is compared to a sword: as, if a man should draw a sword and flourish it about, and should not strike a blow with it, it will doe no harme; even so it is here with the Ministers, little good will they doe if they doe onely explicate; if they doe onely draw out the sword of the Spirit: for unlesse they apply it to the peoples harts particularly, little good may the people expect, little good shall the Minister doe. A common kind of teaching when the Minister doth speake only hoveringly, and in the generall, and never applies the word of God particularly, may be compared to the confused noise that was in the Ship wherein *Jonah* was, when the winds blew, and the sea raged, and a great storm began to arise. The poore Marriners strove with might and maine, and they did endeavour by all meanes possible to bring the ship to the shore; every one cried unto his god and cast their wares into the sea, and all this while *Ionas* was fast asleepe in the ship: but when the Marriners came down and plucked him up, and said, *Arise thou sleeper.,...who art thou? Call upon thy God,* then he was awakened out of his sleepe. The common delivery of the word is like that confused noise: there is matter of heaven, of hell, of grace, of sin spoken of, there is a common noise, and all this while men sit and sleepe carelessly, and never looke about them, but rest secure: but when particular application comes, that shakes a sinner, as the Pilot did *Jonah,* and asks him, What assurance of Gods mercy hast thou? what hope of pardon of sinnes? of life and happinesse hereafter? You are baptized, and so were many that are in hell: you come to Church, and so did many that are in hell: but what is your conversation in the meantime? Is that holy in the sight of God and man?

"When the Ministers of God shake men and take them up on this fashion then they begin to stirre up themselves, and to consider of their estates. This generall and common kind of teaching is like an enditement without a name: if a man should come to the assizes, and make a great exclamation and have no name to his enditement, alas, no man is troubled with it, no man feares it, no man shall receive any punishment by reason of it. So it is with this common kind of preaching, it is an enditement without a name. We arrest none before wee particularly arraigne them before the tribunall of the Lord, and show them these are their sinnes, and that unless they repent and forsake them they shall be damned: for then this would stirre them up, and make them seke to the Lord for mercy: this would rowse them out of their security, and awaken them, and make them say as the Jewes did to Peter and the rest of the Apostles, *Men and brethren what shall wee doe to bee saved?*" [27]

These extracts must suffice. They give a fair average indication of Hooker's style. But they can of course only partially suggest the wonderful variety of pat, homely, forcible illustration, and of sharp, searching, and energetic application, with which the same essential theme of the process of personal religion in the soul is treated in every one of his many volumes, with the single exception which has been specified. They are the product of a mind intent on the characteristic functions of the preacher. And such a preacher was sure of hearers. Such an analyst of human emotions touched men at many points. A son of thunder and a son of consolation by turns, his ministry — whatever the defects or extravagances of his theology — could not have been other than that which all testimony declares it to have been, one of the most powerful of his age.

[1] Appendix Two.
[2] See Goodwin and Nye's preface, and the publisher's announcement to the "Comment upon Christs Last Prayer" and "The Application of Redemption."
[3] Magnalia, i. 315.
[4] Magnalia, i. 314.
[5] Giles Firmin's Real Christian, p. 19.
[6] Hooker's The Soules Preparation, pp. 9, 10.
[7] Shepard's Sincere Convert, p. 150.
[8] Ibid. p. 98.
[9] The Soules Preparation (1632), pp. 12-14.
[10] The Soules Preparation (1632), pp. 150-152.
[11] The Soules Preparation (1632), pp. 182-187.
[12] Magnalia, i. 315.
[13] Prefatory letter to Solomon Stoddard's Guide to Christ.
[14] Firmin's Real Christian, Preface, Introduction, and pp. 107-149.
[15] The Soules Humiliation (1638), pp. 98-100.
[16] The Soules Humiliation (1638), pp. 106, 107.
[17] Ibid. 112.
[18] The Soules Humiliation (1638), pp. 113-115.
[19] Ibid. 115, 116.
[20] Ibid. 114.
[21] The Vnbeleevers Preparing for Christ (1638), pp. 138-140.
[22] The Soules Preparation (1632), pp. 131-136.
[23] Preparing for Christ (1638), part ii. pp. 24-26.
[24] The Soules Exaltation (1638), pp. 122, 123.
[25] The Soules Effectual! Calling (1638), pp. 79, 80.
[26] Comment on Christ's Last Prayer (1656), pp. 319, 320.
[27] The Soules Implantation (1640), pp. 73-77.

Appendix One - Thomas Hooker's Will and Inventory of Estate

The last Will and Testament of Mr. Thomas Hooker, late of Hartford, deceased.

I Thomas Hooker, of Hartford, vppon Connecticutt in New England, being weake in my body, through the tender visitation of the Lord, but of sound and perfect memory, doe dispose of that outward estate I haue beene betrusted withall by him, in manner following: —

I doe giue vnto my sonne John Hooker, my howsing and lands in Hartford, aforesaid, both that which is on the west, and allso that wch is on the east side of the Riuer, to bee inioyed by him and his heires for euer, after the death of my wife, Susanna Hooker, provided hee bee then at the age of one and twenty yeares, it being my will that my said deare wife shall inioye and possess my said howsing and lands during her naturall life: And if shee dye before my sonne John come to the age of one and twenty yeares, that the same bee improued by the overseers of this my will for the maintenance and education of my children not disposed of, according to theire best discretion.

I doe allso giue vnto my sonne John, my library of printed bookes and manuscripts, vnder the limitations and provisoes hereafter expressed. It is my will that my Sonne John deliuer to my sonne Samuell, so many of my bookes as shall bee valued by the ou'seers of this my will to bee worth fifty pounds sterling, or that hee pay him the some of fifty pounds sterling to buy such bookes as may bee vseful to him in the way of his studdyes, at such time as the ouerseers of this my will shall judge meete; but if my sonne John doe not goe on to the perfecting of his studdyes, or shall not giue vpp himselfe to the seruice of the Lord in the worke of the ministry, my will is that my sonne Samuel inioye and possesse the whole library and manuscripts, to his proper vse for euer; onely, it is my will that whateuer manuscripts shall bee judged meete to bee printed, the disposall thereof and advantage that may come thereby I leaue wholly to my executrix; and in case shee departe this life before the same bee judged of and setled, then to my overseers to bee improued by them in theire best discretion, for the good of myne, according to the trust reposed in them. And howeuer I do not forbid my sonne John from seeking and taking a wife in England, yet I doe forbid him from marrying and tarrying there.

I doe giue vnto my sonne Samuell, in case the whole library come not to him, as is before expressed, the sum of seuenty pounds, to bee paid vnto him by my executrix at such time, and in such manner, as shall be judged meetest by the overseers of my will.

I doe allso giue vnto my daughter Sarah Hooker, the sum of one hundred pounds sterhng, to bee paid vnto her by my executrix when she shall marry or come to the age of one and twenty yeares, wch shall first happen; the disposall and further education of her and the rest, I leaue my wife, advising them to attend her councell in the feare of the Lord.

I doe giue vnto the two children of my daughter Joannah Shephard deceased, and the childe of my daughter Mary Newton, to each of them the sum of ten pounds, to bee paid vnto them by my sonne John, within one yeare after hee shall come to the possession and inioyment of my howsings and lands in Hartford, or my sonne Samuell, if by the decease of John, hee come to inioye the same.

I doe make my beloued wife Susannah Hooker, executrix of this my last Will and Testament, and (my just debts being paid,) do giue and bequeath vnto her all my estate and goods, moueable and imouable, not formerly bequeathed by this my will. And I desire my beloued frends Mr. Edward Hopkins and Mr. William Goodwyn, to affoard theire best assistance to my wife, and doe constitute and appoint them the ouerseers of this my will. And it hauing pleased the Lord now to visitt my wife with a sicknes, and not knowing how it may please his Matie to dispose of her, my minde and will is, that in case shee departe this life before shee dispose the estate bequeathed her, my aforesaid beloued frends, Mr. Edward Hopkins and Mr. William Goodwyn, shall take care both of the education and dispose of my children (to whose loue and faithfulnes I commend them,) and of the estate left and bequeathed to my wife, and do committ it to theire best judgment and discretion to manage the said estate for the best good of mine, and to bestow it vppon any or all of them in such a proportion as shall bee most sutable to theire owne apphensions; being willing onely to intimate my desire that they wil deserue best may haue most; but not to limmitt them, but leaue them to the full scope and bredth of their owne judgments; in the dispose whereof, they may haue respect to the forementioned children of my two daughters, if they see meet. It being my full will that what trust I haue comitted to my wife, either in matter of estate, or such manuscripts as shall bee judged fitt to bee printed, in case shee liue not to order the same herselfe, bee wholly transmitted and passed ouer from her to them, for the ends before specified. And for mortallity sake, I doe put power into the hands of the forementioned beloued freinds, to constitute and appoint such other faithfull men as they shall judge meete, (in case they bee depriued of life or libberty to attend the same, in theire owne persons,) to manage, dispose and performe the estate and trust comitted to them, in as full manner as I haue comitted it to them for the same end.

THOMAS HOOKER.

This was declared to bee the last Will and Testament of Mr. Thomas Hooker, the seuenth day of July, 1647. In the presence of

Henry Smith, Samuell Stone, John White.

Appendix Two - Thomas Hooker's Published Works

(Furnished by Dr. J. Hammond Trumbull.)

? [*The Poor Dovting Christian drawne vnto Christ.*
8° *London: Printed in the year* 1629.]
Title from Henry Stevens, — from whom Sabin copied it.

This book does not appear in the Registers of the Stationers' Company until 1637, when (May 6) "The poore doubting Christian drawn to Christ, &c. vpon John the 6th, the 45th [verse], by Master Hooker" was entered for copyright to Mr. [R.] Dawlman and Luke Fawne (*Registers,* iv. 383). Two weeks earlier, "certain Sermons vpon John the 6th, verse the 45th, by T. H.," had been entered to Andrew Crooke (*Ibid.* 381), — which may have been another edition of the same work.

Its *sixth* edition was printed in 1641: —

"The Poore Doubting Christian drawn to Christ. Wherein the main Lets and Hindrances which keep men from coming to Christ are discovered. With especiall Helps to recover God's favor. The Sixth Edition." 12° *London: I. Raworth for Luke Fawne. pp.* (2), 163.

After the 6th, I can trace, in the seventeenth century, only three editions [1652 (*Dr. Williams's Libr. Cat.*); 1659, *J. Macock, for Luke Fawne,* 12°, and 1667, 16° (Am. Antiq. Soc. Catalogue)], before "The Twelfth Edition," 12°, 1700.

The first American edition, with an "Abstract of the author's Life," by the Rev. Thomas Prince, was printed in Boston (for D. Henchman), 1743 (12° *pp.* 14, 144). This edition, with the Life, and an Introduction by Rev. Dr. Edward W. Hooker, was reprinted, Hartford, 1845 (16° *pp.* 165, I).

Sabin (*Dictionary,* no. 32847) says: "This, the earliest and most popular of Hooker's works, first appeared in a collection of sermons entitled 'The Saints' Cordial,' attributed to Sibbs." I have not seen this collection, nor can I find any mention of the edition of 1629, except in H. Stevens's catalogue (and in Sabin), as before noted.

The Sovles Preparation for Christ. Or, A Treatise of Contrition. Wherein is discovered How God breaks the heart and wounds the Soule, in the conversion of a Sinner to Himselfe. *pp.* (8), 258.

This work was entered to R. Dawlman, 29 Oct., 1631, as "The Soules Preparation for Christ, out of Acts 2, 37, and Luke 15, by *F. H.,*" — as the printed Register (iv. 263) has it, by a clerical error for T. H. One third of the copyright was assigned, 14 Oct., 1634, to R. Allott, and by Allott's widow, 1 July, 1637, to Legatt and Andrew Crooke.

The Eqvall Wayes of God: Tending to the Rectifying of the Crooked Wayes of Man. The Passages whereof are briefly and clearly drawne from the sacred Scriptures. By T. H.

4° *London; for John Clarke,* 1632. *pp.* (8), 40.

Entered to J. Clarke, 6 Dec, 1631 (*Registers,* iv. 267). The prefatory address. To the Christian Reader, is signed T. H., showing that the publication was authorized by the author.

[*An Exposition of the Lord's Prayer.* By T, H. 1638.] Entered, as above, to Mr. [R.] Dawlman, 5 Sept., 1637 (*Stat. Registers,* iv. 392). It is advertised, as published, in a list of Mr, Hooker's books, prefixed to (the 4th edition of) "The Soules Preparation," etc., 1638. The Bodleian Catalogue has: *Heaven's Treasury opened,* in a faithfull Exposition of the Lord's Prayer, 8° *Lond.* 1645 and Sabin has that title and date nearly (no. 32839), with "fruitful" in place of "faithfull," and adding: "with a Treatise on the Principles of Religion;" but marking the size as 4to. The Bodleian has, as a separate title: "An Exposition of the Principles of Religion," 8° 1645, — in the list of Hooker's works.

The Sovles Humiliation. 4° *London, for A. Crooke,* 1637. Entered (as, by T. H.) Feb. 28, 1636-7, to A. Crooke, by whom one half the copyright was assigned to P. Nevill, 13 March, 1637-8 (*Registers,* iv. 374, 412). The licenser's imprimatur is dated Oct. 10 and Dec. 6, 1637.

The Souls Implantation. A Treatise containing, The Broken Heart, on Esay 57. 15. The Preparation of the Heart, on Luke i. 17. The Soules Ingraffing into Christ, on Mai. 3. i. Spirituall Love and Joy, on GaL 5. 22. By T. H. 4° *R. Young, sold by F. Clifton,* 1637. pp. (2), 266.

Entered 22 Apr., 1637, to Young and Chfton {Registers, iv. 382). Another, much improved edition, under the title —

The Soules Implantation into the Naturall Olive. By T. H. Carefully corrected, and much enlarged. With a Table of the Contents prefixed.

4° *R. Young, sold by F. Clifton,* 1640. *pp.* (6), 320.

The Sermon on Spiritual *Joy,* on Habak. 3. 17, 18, is added in this edition, and the preceding Sermon, on Spiritual *Love,* was printed from larger and more accurate notes.

The Sovles Ingrafting into Christ. By T. H.

4° *J. H[aviland]* for A. Crooke, 1637. pp. (2), 30.

The text is Mai. 3. i. It is one of three "Sermons...by T. H." entered to Crooke, 22 July, 1637 (*Registers,* iv. 390). Another edition of it makes part of "The Soules Implantation" 1637. See the next preceding title.

The Sovles Effectuall Calling to Christ. By T. H.

4° *J. H.[aviland]* or A. Crooke, 1637. *pp.* (2), 33-668.

Entered to A. Crooke, 21 Apr., 1637, as "certain Sermons upon John the 6th, verse the 4Sth, by T. H." {Register, iv. 381.) Usually bound with "The Sovles Ingrafting," with which its paging is continuous; but also published separately (though without change of paging), with a second title prefixed, —

The Sovles Vocation or Effectval Calling to Christ. By T. H.

With a Table of Contents (11 leaves), and in imprint, the date 1638.

[*The Soules Possession of Christ:* upon Romans 13:4, Acts 16:31, Psal. 51: 16, John 7: 37, 2 Kings 2: 12, 1 Peter 5:5, Zeph. 2:3. By T. H.] 8°, 1638.

So entered to [R.] Dawlman, 13 Nov. 1637. The Bodleian Catalogue has: The Soules Possession of Christ: whereunto is annexed a Funeral Sermon on

2 Kings ii. 12. 8° Lond. 1638. Spitituall Mimition: a funeral Sermon, on 2 Kings ii. 12. By T. H. 8° Lord. 1638" (Bodl, Cat.), appears to have been also published separately.

The Sovles Exaltation. A Treatise containing The Soules Vnion with Christ, on i Cor. 6. 17. The Soules Benefit from Vnion with Christ, on i Cor. i. 30. The Soules Justification, on 2 Cor. 5. 21. By T. H.

4° *J. Haviland, for Andr. Crooke,* 1638 . pp. (16), 311.

8 April, 1637, [12] "Sermons ... by T. H." were entered to Andrew Crooke, — the text of each being named (*Registers,* iv. 380). These sermons were made up into three volumes, under the titles, "The Soules Exaltation" (3), "Four Treatises," etc. (3), and "The Vnbeleevers Preparing for Christ" (5), — all published in 1638.

The Vnbeleevers Preparing for Christ. Luke i. 17. By T. H.

4° *T. Cotes for Andr. Crooke,* 1638. pp. (4), 204, (4); 119, (4).

Six sermons. The first five selected from the "Sermons by T. H.," entered to A. Crooke, 8 April, 1637; the last (on John 6. 44), one of "certain sermons ... by T. H.," entered to the same publisher, 22 July, 1637 {Registers, iv. 380, 390).

Four godly and learned Treatises: viz.: The Carnall Hypocrite. The Churches Deliverances. The Deceitfulness of Sinne. The Benefit of Afflictions. By T. H.

12° *A. Crooke,* 1638.

(Prince Library and Bodleian Catalogues.) Probably four of the (12) Sermons by T. H. entered to Crooke, 8 April, 1637. Among "several Treatises by this Author" advertised by Cooke, 1638, are "Sermons on Judges 10. 23; on Psalms 119. 29; on Proverbs 1.28,29; and on 2 Tim. 3. 5." These sermons are included in the collection entered 8 April, except the third, which is one of four entered to the same publisher, 22 July, 1637. (Crooke assigned half the copyright of these "Four Treatises" to Wm. Wethered, i Sept., 1638.)

? [*The Garments of Salvation* first putt off" by the Fall of our first Parents. Secondly, putt on again by the Grace of the Gospel. By T. H. 1639?]

Entered, 6 May, 1639, to R. Young and Fulke Clifton (*Registers,* iv. 465). Mr. Arber queries, "? by Thomas Hooker." Certainly intended to *pass* for his. I have not been able to find a copy of it.

The Christians Two Chiefe Lessons, Viz. Selfe-Deniall, and Selfe-Tryall. As also. The Priviledge of Adoption and Triall thereof. In three Treatises on the Texts following: Viz. Matt. 16. 24. 2 Cor. 13. 5. lohn i. 12, 13. By T. H.

4° T. B. *for P. Stephens and C. Meredith,* 1640. *pp.* (24), 303.

An "Epistle Dedicatory" to "the Honourable and truly Religious Lady, the Lady Anne Wake," is subscribed, Z. S. [Rev. Zechariah Symmes of Charlestown?], who "had taken some paines in the perusall and transcribing" the copy "after it came into the Printers hands," and "one that was inwardly acquainted with the Authour [Thomas Shepard?] hath laboured with me in this taske."

"Treatise or certaine Sermons 'of Selfe Denyall' upon Matthew 16. 24 and 25 verses, by T. H.," was entered 15 Dec., 1638, to Stevens and Meredith (*Registers,* iv. 448). The completed work, with the title as above, was entered to the same partners, 15 Oct., 1639 (*ibid.* 483).

[*The Patterne of Perfection* exhibited in God's Image on Adam and God's Covenant with him, on Genesis i. 26. Whereunto is added, *An Exhortacion to redeeme tyme* for recovering our losses in the premises on Ephesians, 5. 16. Also *certaine Queries* touching a true and sound Christian, by T. H.]

This title was entered to Mr. [R.] Young and Fulke Clifton, 19 Feb., 1638-9 (*Registers,* iv. 455). Published (in a second edition?), 1640, 8° (*Bodl. Cat.*).

The Danger of Desertion: or A Far well Sermon of Mr. *Thomas Hooker,* Somtimes Minister of God's Word at *Chainsford* in *Essex;* but now of *New* England. Preached immediately before his departure out of old England. — Together with Ten Particular rules to be practised every day by converted Christians.

4° G. *M. for Geo. Edwards,* 1641. pp. (4), 29.

Text, Jerem. 14. 9. A Second edition was printed the same year (Prince Libr. Cat.). A MS. note by the Rev. T. Prince attributes the "Ten Rules" to the Rev. E. Reyner.

The Faithful Covenanter. A Sermon preached at the Lecture in Dedham in Essex. By that excellent servant of Jesus Christ, in the work of the Gospel, Mr. Tho. Hooker, late of Chelmsford; now in New-England. Very usefull in these times of Covenanting with God. Psal. 78. vers. 9, [10, 36, 37: 8 lines].

4° *Christopher Meredith,* 1644. *pp.* (2), 43. Text from Deut. 29. 24, 25. Printed from the notes of some hearer — and without the author's knowledge — as "very useful in these times" of subscribing the "Solemn League and Covenant."

"? [*An Exposition of the Principles of Religion.*

8° 1645.]

Title from the Bodleian Catalogue. I have not seen it.

The Saints Guide, in three Treatises on Gen. vi. 13, [3,] Rom. i. 18, and Ps. i. 3. 8° *Lond.* 1645.

Bodl. Catalogue. "Three Sermons upon these Texts (vizt.) Romans i. 18, Genesis 6. 3, Psalms i. 3, by T. H." were entered to John Stafford, 10 Aug., 1638 {Stat. Reg., iv. 428); but I can trace no earlier edition than that of 1645.

? [The Immortality of the Sotile. The Excellencie of Christ Jesus, treated on. Wherein the faithfull people of God may find comfort for their Souls. By T. H. Published according to Order. 4° 1646. pp. (2), 21.]

Title from Sabin's Dictionary (no. 32841), where it is attributed to Hooker.

[*Heautonaparnumenos:* or a *Treatise of Self-Denyall.* Intended for the Pulpit; but now committed to the Presse for the Publike Benefit. By Thomas Hooker. London, Wilson for Rich. Royston, 1646.

Title from Sabin (no. 32840), who evidently had not seen the book, for he does not give the size or number of pages. I am confident this *title* is not (our) Thomas Hooker's: but the book may be a bookseller's make-up from "The Christians Two Chiefe Lessons," etc., published in 1640.

Posthumous.

A Survey of the Summe of Church-Discipline. Wherein, The Way of the Churches of New-England is warranted out of the Word, etc. ... By Tho. Hooker, late Pastor of the Church at *Hartford* upon *Connecticut* in N. E.

4° *A. M. for John Bellamy,* 1648. *pp.* (36); Part 1. *pp.* 139 (1 blk.), 185-296; Part II. p*p.* 90; Part III. pp. 46; Part IV. *pp.* 59.

The author's preface (18 pp.) is followed by an Epistle to the Reader (4 pp.) subscribed by Edward Hopkins and William Goodwin, Hartford, 28 Oct., 1647: a Poem "in obitum viri Doctissimi Thomae Hookeri," by Samuel Stone; others by John Cotton and E. Rogers: and a further commendation to the reader by Thomas Goodwin, April 17, 1648.

This work, it appears, was "finished, and sent near two years" earlier, to be printed; but the copy "was then buried in the rude waves of the vast Ocean, with many precious Saints, in their passage hither." Mr. Hooker reluctantly consented to prepare another copy for the press, but "before the full transcribing, he was translated from us to be ever with the Lord."

To some copies of the work, John Cotton's "The Way of Congregational Churches cleared" was appended, and a general title, including both works, prefixed to the volume. Mr. Cotton's treatise continues the answers to Rutherford, begun by Mr. Hooker in Part I. Chap. 10, of the Survey. That chapter ends on p. 139, the next page is blank, and Chapter 11 begins on the next page following, numbered 185, with a new signature. It may have been the intention of the editors to incorporate Mr. Cotton's work with Hooker's, in this division of the Survey, or the former may have been substituted for Hooker's unfinished notes.

The Covenant of Grace opened: wherein These particulars are handled; viz. i. What the Covenant of Grace is, 2. What the Seales of the Covenant are, 3. Who are the Parties and Subjects fit to receive these Seales. From all which Particulars Infants Baptisme is fully proved and vindicated. Being severall Sermons preached at Hartford in New-England. By that Reverend and faithfull Minister of the Gospel, Mr. Thomas Hooker.

4° *G. Dawson,* 1649. *pp.* (2), 85.

The Saints Dignitie and Dutie. Together with The Danger of Ignorance and Hardnesse. Delivered in severall Sermons: By that Reverend Divine, Thomas Hooker, Late Preacher in New-England.

4° *G. D*[*awson*], *for Francis Eglesfield,* 1651. pp. (12), 246.

Seven sermons: i. *The Gift of Gifts:* or, The End why Christ gave Himself (*Titus* 2. 14): 2. *The Blessed Inhabitant:* or, The Benefit of Christs being in Beleevers (Rom. 8. 10); 3. *Grace Magnified:* or the Priviledges of those that are under Grace (Rom. 6. 14); 4. *Wisdomes Attendants:* or The Voice of Christ to be obeyed {Prov. 8. 32): 5. *The Activitie of Faith:* or, Abraham's Imitators {Rom. 4. 12): 6. *Culpable Ignorance:* or the Danger of Ignorance under Meanes (Is. 27:11): 7. *Wilful Hardnesse:* or the Means of Grace Abused (*Prov.* 29. i). Each sermon has a full title page, with imprint as in the general title; and probably each was sold separately, though the paging is continuous.

The preface, signed T. S. [Thomas Shepard], shows that this volume was prepared for the press by Mr. Hooker's son-in-law.

A Comment upon Christ's Last Prayer in the Seventeenth of John. Wherein is opened, The Vnion Beleevers have with God and Christ, and the Glorious Priviledges thereof. ... By ... Mr. Thomas Hooker, *etc...*Printed from the Author's own Papers, ...and attested to be such...by Thomas Goodwin and Philip Nye.

4° *Peter Cole,* 1656. *pp.* (26), 532.

Half-title, on p. 1: "Mr. Hooker's Seventeenth Book made in New-England." A series of sermons on John 17. 20-26, preached, at the administration of the Lord's Supper, in the last years of Mr. Hooker's pastorate.

The numbering of the volume as "Mr. Hooker's Seventeenth Book" has given some trouble to the bibliographers. Of a collection of seventeen "books" — each comprising one or more sermons — sent to England for publication, the first *eight* were published together by P. Cole, 1656 [and 1657], under the general title of "The Application of Redemption," etc.; and two others, the *ninth* and *tenths* made a second volume under the same title. Six others (the *eleventh* to the *sixteenth,* inclusive) were announced by Cole, in 1656, as "now printing, in two volumes," but I find no evidence that they were ever published. The *seventeenth* "and last" (as Cole announced it) was "A Comment upon Christ's Prayer," etc.

The Application of Redemption. By the Effectual Work of the Word, and Spirit of Christ, for the bringing home of lost Sinners to God. [The first Eight Books.] ...By...Thomas Hooker, etc. Printed from the Authour's Papers, ...with ... an Epistle by Thomas Goodwin, and Philip Nye. 8° 1657. pp. (46), 451.

The title and collation are from Sabin: but the Catalogue of the Red Cross (Dr. Williams's) Library mentions two editions of 1656, one in octavo, the other in quarto.

The Application of Redemption., etc. The *Ninth* and *Tenth* Books ...Printed from the Author's Papers, Written with his own hand. And attested to be such, in an Epistle, By Thomas Goodwin and Philip Nye.

4° *Peter Cole,* 1657. *pp.* (22), 702, (30).

The same. The Second Edition.

4° *Peter Cole, 1*659. *pp.* (22), 702, (30).

The prefatory epistle of Goodwin and Nye gives, in brief, the history of this work, and, incidentally, of many of the earlier editions of Hooker's sermons. "Many parts and pieces of this Author, upon this argument, sermon-wise, preach'd by him here in England, ...having been taken by an unskilful hand, which, upon his recess into those remoter parts of the World, was bold without his privity or consent to print and publish them, ...his genuine meaning was diverted...from the clear draft of his own notions and intentions. ... In these Treatises, thou hast his Heart from his own Hand, his own Thoughts drawn by his own Pencil," *etc.* He had preached more briefly of this subject, first, while a Fellow and Catechist at Emmanuel College, and again, many years after, more largely, at Chelmsford, — *"the product of which was those books of Sermons that have gone utider his name,* — and last of all, now in New-England."

www.ingramcontent.com/pod-product-compliance
Ingram Content Group UK Ltd.
Pitfield, Milton Keynes, MK11 3LW, UK
UKHW041930190726
13854UKWH00004B/1537